JOY IN PLAIN SIGHT

JOY IN PLAIN SIGHT

STORIES AND ESSAYS CELEBRATING
WONDER IN THE ORDINARY

KATYA DAVYDOVA

NEW DEGREE PRESS

JOY IN PLAIN SIGHT

Stories and Essays Celebrating Wonder in the Ordinary

ISBN   979-8-88504-111-9 *Paperback*

979-8-88504-738-8 *Kindle Ebook*

979-8-88504-217-8 *Ebook*

Appreciate everything, even the ordinary...
Especially the ordinary.

PEMA CHODRON

CONTENTS

INTRODUCTION

——

We should've been dead, really. A grotesque meet-cute of two cars, barreling down a tar ribbon at precisely the stated speed limit, concluding in a violent kiss of twisted metal.

Head-on collisions usually end up in one of two ways: death or near-death. When the passengers of both cars—my dear friend and I and the other gentleman—walked out of the wreckage, we were the lucky ones.

Despite months-long rehab and hobbling around with a slight grimace, I bounced back. My bone bruises healed, and new scars made their home on my body. The remaining smolder was the nightly replay of the microseconds before the crash, a dark lullaby before turbulent sleep.

For some, toeing the line with death can be a beautiful, meaningful, transformative experience: an opportunity to begin anew and shed all the built-up bullshit that once mattered so much.

For me, survival was more a matter of fact.

The crash happened on a Saturday morning in September of my senior year of college. By Sunday, these thoughts raced through my head:

Great, Katya, we see you're still here. Congratulations. Now, you've got job applications due next week, your thesis review in two months, and, oh, you're still going to limp a few miles across campus to lead that group meeting tomorrow, right?

Don't get me wrong; I was delighted I was still here. Part of my human makeup was—and still is—I was generally happy to be alive. In high school, I'd joined the Optimists Club and was known for being a walking smiley face brimming with silver linings. And I had *so* much to be thankful for.

When I was seven, my parents had won a green card visa lottery to emigrate from Uzbekistan to pursue the American dream. Every year, the US Department of State chooses fifty-five thousand people from millions of citizens in underrepresented countries to apply for residency. We were three of the lucky ones.

As an only child, I was flying on the wings of hope, soaring from my parents' sacrifices to the faraway lands of a better life. And so, I became good at being good—it's what was expected of me.

Perhaps you know someone with a similar thread. Perhaps you know it yourself.

Over time, with the accolades came perfectionism and the need to continually strive, imposed by external expectations, but more viciously, by me.

I remember sobbing in the dim staircase of our home one night during junior year. My head burned from trying, and failing, to understand physics problems in the textbooks and worksheets scattered all over the living room table.

"Let's run a few more practice problems before your test tomorrow, and you should really get some sleep, Katya," my mom soothed, pointing to my room upstairs.

It was close to 1 a.m., but I had to keep going.

I graduated from my magnet high school with straight A's, except for that one C+ in physics. Ironically, the only equation that stuck was $F=ma$.

The more effort and energy I put into school, the better and faster the outcomes. There was no emergency brake.

So the norm was to continue to apply force and watch my world speed up through a double major and a minor in college. Study the psychology and cognitive science of human behavior, and excel there, too. Continue achieving—through more late nights brimming with research and leadership and sports—and graduate with highest excellence as conferred by others.

Feel the force of a near-fatal car crash during the last year of university yet continue accelerating because that's what the equation states.

On graduation day, my mother hugged me after I waded through the sea of faces, diploma in hand.

"You did it! Aren't you proud of yourself?" she asked.

"I mean, yeah," I said, checking my phone to see what was on the docket for the rest of the day.

Well of course you did it! You had to.

Later that day at our family celebratory dinner, she handed me a symbolic gift.

A compass.

But what are you doing next?

This last question remained a theme throughout my twenties. My goal was to find the next, tallest branch in the tree of life, overprepare, and jump to catch it.

Remember, I heard over and over again, *there's always a higher branch, and you have to keep climbing.*

As my career blossomed, I jumped from branch to branch with ease. When my first adult job in healthcare consulting became unbearably boring—with many of my twenty-something coworkers plotting our escape from the corporate cubicle farm—I switched cities.

One hundred miles south of the nation's bustling capital, I dashed from my day job in higher education, to an hourlong workout, to leading my local Toastmasters club, to grabbing a Tuesday night special at my favorite beer joint—an opportunity to observe and write about solitary regulars and boisterous newcomers.

Back at home after fourteen hours away, I'd drink in a nightcap of discourses on organizational development for graduate school.

"Do you ever take a break?" my friend asked.

It was our monthly phone call, and I'd specifically planned it for one of my long runs that week.

"Hm, I can't, really. There's just too much to do."

The same month I finished grad school, I gave my two weeks' notice at work and began preparing for a cross-country move to Los Angeles. While I loved the cohesive community in my cozy mountain town, I craved newness, adventure, speed.

I suppose a part of me wanted to live more colorfully by that famous physics equation, $F=ma$. I packed the essentials into every nook and cranny of my car and sped westward on Interstate 70. My force, up to this point, was proportional to the whirlwind of career pivots, promotions, and a drive to continue accelerating.

The world, too, grew increasingly complex and disorienting each year. We sped into the era of the attention economy, where the most valued and sought-after commodity was what we paid attention to.

I'd get whiplash from cycling through emails, text messages, and virtual shoulder taps. For years, I'd beg my heated laptop to keep grinding at night as I swapped out work tabs for whatever was my side project of the month. Every minute of my day had to have some productive purpose. And yet, I was constantly distracted by another shiny idea, sound, or thought.

In my career in organizational development—making work better for humans—I learned our jobs were just as distracting and pernicious. In a given hour, an average employee gets interrupted once every three minutes. Moreover, almost half of those interruptions are self-inflicted. *We're literally self-sabotaging our own attention span!*

We were drowning from having to swim the ocean of stimuli, trying to catch each singular, pounding wave.

How curious, then, that while making work more fun and engaging for others, I found myself feeling drained at the end of the workday. Perhaps you might have felt a similar exhaustion, too.

And then, when the world economies ground to a halt during the global pandemic, I felt like I *still* could not get off this hamster wheel. A season of slowness felt like a season of ambiguous force. I had mass, and I expelled energy, but one question lingered: *What was I doing next?*

During the height of lockdown, I frequently replayed my car accident, remembering how there had been no choice and no chance to slow down and recover afterward. I needed to force my way forward.

Almost a decade later, with millions dying, parts of the world continued to churn. Organizations hoped to squeeze out every ounce of productivity from employees and wondered why they smelled burnout. During the season of ten-hour workdays stacked with side gigs and other commitments, I wondered, too, if I could ever extinguish the smoldering.

How could I stop feeling burnt out and start feeling more whole?

How could we as a society garner more space?

If I told you I'd found the answer, you would likely read this book. But I'm hopeful you will read it for another reason—because I don't have the answer.

What I *did* find were hummingbirds playing without a care in the world. A ripe lemon tree decorating the yard of the charred remains of a house. Vibrant California fuchsia, larkspur, yarrow blooming week after week, as if the most precious thing they could do with their existence was to drink up sunshine and radiate outward.

While the months paradoxically slipped by with unnerving force because all else was at a standstill, I'd experiment with embodying the world's stillness, too. All too often, I'd look up from my screens, and a month, then two, would vanish.

Without anywhere to go, I'd lose myself on loops around the neighborhood, purposefully walking—not running—to seek out ways to slow down time. By leaving my footprints on familiar sidewalks, I began to shift my attention to what was immediately at hand, beneath my feet, in front of my eyes. It gave me the space to drift languidly backward and forward in time.

I'd revel in people. Bask in the warmth of a stranger's crinkled eyes, catching their smile beneath the mask. Grin to myself when I was privy to a private moment of the couple just ahead, pausing to steal a kiss.

After every walk, I'd come home refreshed, full of space brimming with details.

And it was these very details I kept coming back to. The phoenix lemon tree, much like the green sprouts carpeting wildfire-ravaged mountains of the Angeles National Forest. The freckles on my partner's skin. The conversation about candles with a lady at the grocery store. The way present human idiosyncrasies dance with memories of the past and how absolutely, astoundingly, curiously wonderful the little things are.

These small moments that hiccup the day-to-day.

I didn't grow up around religion and believe it is a sheer, yet magnificent, coincidence that we experience a handful of decades of being alive—that we *get to* experience them at all. The atoms that live in us—the ones that *are* us—have been recycled through millennia and will continue to reincarnate in future forms.

To me, life has no inherent meaning. *We exist. We die. That's it.*

Guided by philosophers and writers, I realized every tangible success like doing well in school, moving up in my career, getting raises, grinding through months of nonstop daily workouts—none of that really matters when I'm dead. Sure, I'm proud of my efforts, but are they the secret ingredients to a meaningful life?

Like Viktor Frankl in *Man's Search for Meaning,* I believe life has meaning when we *give* it meaning. Meaning arises when we tie together disparate threads to form a quilt, a mosaic of moments. Ultimately, while we are here, we can *weave* meaning into a beautiful existence.

And what happens when some of us—the lucky ones—get a second chance at existing? How do we make sense of borrowed time?

For many of us, the weeks and months and years slip far faster than we'd like.

So the question I ask you is this:

How do we slow down time and make space for anything to mean anything at all?

My hypothesis is meaning is made in the *pause* of those moments. It's being so resoundingly present we can go outside ourselves, push our own pause button, slip back in to taste the now.

And then, of course, write about it.

To me, writing is the art of paying attention.

And paying attention is particularly difficult to do because we are distracted by three million minefields anywhere we turn, yet we get lost in the blurry sameness of days.

But just like uncovering an ecosystem of fauna beneath a carpet of decaying leaves, or an orchestra of birds shattering the silence of a foggy mountain, so much joy and delight can be found in the ordinary. It's that smile of a stranger. It's being witness to a couple's love.

And that joy—those little sparkles within each day—is *always* there.

Our job is to deliberately search for them, and pause to revel when we find them.

My friend Morgan once shared with me a brilliant, paraphrased quote by Kurt Vonnegut:

"There's a reason we're called human beings, not human doings."

I've been carrying this mantra around for years, and it gets more relevant with each passing month. *How do I get off this hamster wheel and simply be? How do I break the cycle of self-imposed productivity and drive for achievement and learn to enjoy a minute of rest?*

While I don't have the answer—because you might have your own—what I so optimistically want to share is my own experiment: I decided to punctuate the closing of a decade of living with an exclamation point instead of the usual ellipsis. For that final year, I wanted to embark on a challenge to test my own limits.

I explored plans for crafting my own Happiness Project, à la human nature writer Gretchen Rubin, or making some kind of yearlong art, or mastering a new skill every month until the next milestone birthday.

Classic human doing pattern. Perhaps this resonates with you too.

In the end, it came down to seeking the answer to the reason we're human *beings*—all the joys, sorrows, sameness, variety, and utter, magnificent absurdity that is a human life.

This collection of stories and essays is my own attempt to pause in the moments that make us *be* and uncover the sparkles that shine in the ordinary.

I hope you find your own sparkle too.

Here's to seeking that joy in plain sight.

LEMONADE

———

In the heat of the first pandemic summer in Los Angeles, I watched a house magnificently burn.

During that same season when wildfires raged, flames engulfed buildings throughout the city. Negligent individuals set fires to vacant homes and structures, dousing the city in oranges and reds and grays to match the backdrop of the mountains.

One Saturday morning I awoke to the smell of deep smoke and hopped on the Citizen app to dutifully investigate a safety alert in my area. Citizen had become a weird obsession during the lockdown, where my anxiety was both fueled and oddly comforted by scrolling through all the local crime. Headlines like "Three suspects involved in shooting" instilled in me both tremendous gratitude I was safe and also a layer of fear for the victims. Others, like "Man wielding bong," provided mirth at the ridiculousness of what the app reported. We were living in strange times.

Even stranger that morning was realizing the connection between what I smelled and what I saw on the screen. Firefighters were en route to a structure fire a few blocks from my own place. I had to see for myself.

On the scene, tangerine danced with sable in billowing plumes. An acrid blanket hung in the air, heavy. Onlookers gathered around the fire trucks, staring in awe or recording the footage I'd seen on Citizen just a few minutes before.

There was an eerie calm about the whole dance, where the firefighters and neighbors seemed to understand the inevitability of what was to come. They glided in deliberate yet fluid motions.

I watched as the firefighters worked in unison. Grab the hose, hoist it up, and hold.

I watched, too, as the onlookers swayed in their curiosity. Grab the phone, cameras up, and hold.

"Do you know what happened?" I asked a man in his thirties standing by his partner recording the flames on her phone.

"Oh, probably some arson. Place has been vacant for months. Shame though." He shrugged.

"Yeah, shame." A pause.

"I hope everyone's okay," I offered.

"Yeah."

A few minutes of silence ticked by. I felt uncomfortably out of place even among the crowd of onlookers. Rubbernecking at someone else's misfortune, even at an empty shell of a house belonging to no one, still felt perversely intimate. Lacking a way to offer any sort of support, I slinked away, back to the safety of my apartment.

Over the next hour, I continued fueling the flames of my anxiety by repeatedly refreshing Citizen. A little virtual rubbernecking, from the comfort of my own home. *How morbid.*

At last, a bit of good news flashed on my phone screen: The blaze was gone. Firefighters left. The smell abated. Just as I sighed a breath of relief, the app pinged again.

A wildfire was devouring acres somewhere to the north, in the parched San Gabriel Mountains. A different kind of blaze was spreading: a cancer to nature.

I alerted my roommate about the grim start to fire season. We'd both been in LA for a few years, so the yearly cycle of burning wasn't new. However, the gravity of the inevitable outcome never felt easier to bear.

"I hope everyone's okay."

"Yeah, me too."

Later that afternoon, when I sat down to work, I traced a line through a thin layer of soot on my desk, the product of leaving my windows open to combat summer heat. While the fire was extinguished, the memory burned on.

Summer burned on, too. Weekday mornings started with a daily stroll around the neighborhood as a way to feel grounded against the backdrop of a particularly stressful work season.

Within a month of the first lockdowns in March 2020, our company announced a merger with significant layoffs. On the afternoon of the announcement, I remember searching colleagues in Slack, dismayed at how many had the gray *"deactivated"* by their names. *Who was next?*

While I felt fortunate to survive several dissolutions of the teams I'd come to know in the following months, I was now running on fumes trying to survive arduously long workdays. My shoulders worked their way up to my ears. I cried more often than ever. I needed to find solace in something.

So, every morning, before plunging into hours of staring at a screen, I'd embark on my daily pilgrimage, passing the same ordinary scenes.

I'd mentally remark on the houses and apartment buildings I had passed so many times before. *Oh, here's Tiffany's place, with her thirteen-year-old dog and even older, outdoor Siamese tomcat. I wonder where he's roaming now. Ah, look at that! Coming up on the fig tree that never seems to ripen. Up ahead are the crushed mulberries making their graves on hot pavement.*

I'd see the same cycle of trotting dogs, waving neighbors, succulents basking in post-dawn glow, and that house. That carnage, those lanky limbs, charred but still standing, held together by memory of what once was.

The house was fenced off by a discordant pattern of chain link, and for a few weeks after the fire, a bitter cloud would linger as I walked past. It was a sight for sore eyes and sore noses. Against the turquoise sky, the black wooden pillars whispered, *Remember me. Remember my death by negligence. Remember my ancestors, burning now, still.*

And it was a sobering reminder of the forests dying by fire in the mountains. Firefighters flocked to the smoky hills, residents fled, and a deep layer of soot covered the smoldering remains.

By late fall, the oppressive heat gave way to some semblance of breathability, and my morning walks felt more enjoyable. I was no longer burning up myself. While work hadn't cooled off completely—I was still pulling wicked hours and feeling the sting of decreased social interaction due to pandemic precautions—there was a smell of hope in the air. Something about the changing of seasons invited a rush of newness.

My walking routes remained unchanged, anchored in one sliver of stability amid the chaos of the raging pandemic. This was my routine, and I could count on the trotting dogs, waving neighbors, even the burnt house as markers of consistency. Walking past that house was no longer jarring to the senses. It had seamlessly woven itself into the quotidian quilt.

Because it was cooler, I decided to add afternoon walks to my routine as a chance to get out of my tiny apartment and invigorate my days with whatever color I could. I saw the same scenes dozens *more* times, sidewalks well-worn with my invisible footprints.

On one of those ambling, post-lunch walks, deep into an audiobook, a glint of yellow suddenly caught my gaze. I narrowed my eyes, furrowed my brows, and looked fully up. There, against the backdrop of black, stood a small lemon tree, sagging under the weight of twenty ripe, yellow orbs.

How had I not noticed this tree, *this life,* sprouting right from the ashes on the last hundred walks past? As I peered closer through the chain link fence, I saw the trunk rooted in the richness of nourishing soil, emerald leaves stretching endlessly upward and outward, and the lemons themselves—bulbous, healthy, unbelievably juicy.

This was life rising from death.

Nature's own lemonade.

A year after that first pandemic summer, I treated myself to a lengthy jaunt through the mountains, a new trail within an hour of my new place. Especially after a tumultuous year, the act of hiking in uncharted territories close to my new apartment brought a sense of groundedness—a new life-taking root.

The trail was a rollercoaster on legs, and I reveled in the narrowness of the single track bordered by stark contrasts of green and black. If I squinted hard enough through the smog draping over the city, I could see the general vicinity of both my apartments, old and new.

Deep in these mountains, wildfires, too, had raged. The earth was now cool from last summer, yet ever on the precipice of a blaze from arson or a gust of wind. I walked through alien land, through layers of soot and ash, and looked on past charred tree stumps and the nothingness wildfires leave behind.

On one particular portion of the trail, I bent down to survey the carnage at my feet. My gaze fanned to either side of the blackened earth and was immediately drawn to a spark of color.

Emerald, green.

Tiny leaves unfurling from their burned log of a home, reaching upward and outward to kiss the azure spread above.

After death, life.

The mountains reincarnate themselves in yearly rhythms, from carcasses to newness, from black to rainbowed hues. As I trekked through those ridges, I thought about how humans, too, ride the cycle of new to old, old to new.

For me, that meant putting out old fires and rebuilding. It meant leaving a stressful job to step into a new one that gave me much of the passion, energy, and meaning that working during a merger and a pandemic had stripped away.

It meant pulling myself out of a creative rut and writing this book about finding the joys in plain sight. It meant saying a rather wistful but triumphant goodbye to my cramped apartment and moving westward to brighter pastures—or city streets, at least.

It meant leaving the neighborhood with that burned-down house and adopting a new daily walking habit, where neighbors waved while walking their dogs, where figs burst with ripeness and made a sticky carpet on the pavement below.

Most curiously, it meant moving into a home with a lemon tree in the backyard, in all its emerald and golden magnificence.

WELCOME TO THE
NEIGHBORHOOD

———

My partner and I had just moved into a new place together, the one with the lemon tree in the backyard. Our new neighborhood is quite lovely, blooming with the flowers and charm of a vibrant part of town, about thirty minutes south of where wildfires burned in the Los Angeles mountains.

Down the palm-tree-lined street are sturdy, rectangular edifices housing several sets of tenants, usually in two-story, multi-family homes. Originally built in the 1920s, this neighborhood is now home to thirty-somethings with roommates, families young and old, and quite a few pet owners.

No two buildings look alike; some have Spanish-style windows, others have sprawling balconies, others still have walled-in gardens and patios. Walking past plots of watered lawns or decadent succulents, we see elements of colonial, art deco, and Tudor styles. Taken altogether, these houses are a welcoming mosaic of colors and designs.

There is, however, one feature that unifies them all.

"It's as if God shat out a giant brick." That's my best description to visiting friends of the houses in our neighborhood. Giant bricks: those behemoth, rectangular structures that have stood the test of time—and have lived to tell the tale.

Now, because our particular, portly, pink building has sat on its corner lot for almost a century, it's really seen it all. Not only does it provide a warm residence for each pair of its residents, but it also contains a bounty of other hidden quirks and treasures that make one feel right at home.

For example, this building makes it so we no longer need an alarm clock.

Imagine: The sun has just stretched its first rays over the horizon, and the day is about to begin. All is silent in the neighborhood, except for a sudden onslaught of grunts and groans coming from a man courtesy of his girlfriend.

Which man?

Well, there are plenty in our quadplex to choose from!

There are Chris and Philip, two men in their fifties rooming below us. Chris' friendly girlfriend, Diana, spends the night several times a week, so that is possibility number one.

Next to us are Brian and Bill, two dudes in their thirties, one of whom has his girlfriend occasionally stays over on the weekends. Usually, they are out exploring the California mountains, but still remain potential contenders.

That leaves Jim and John below Brian and Bill, another two guys in their twenties and thirties who'd only become roommates through convenience and who, conveniently for us, haven't brought over any overnight guests.

Speaking of convenience, our neighbors are thoughtful enough to ensure we never miss a sunrise. *Why would one choose to wake up to a gentle, xylophone tune, when primal screams will jolt open your eyes faster than you can reach for your phone to silence the music? Why even have a phone at all?*

Why, indeed. That is the question of the hour—because I ask myself that groggily every hour. I get the sense my other neighbors don't really mind too much, since all of us have been waking up to the same human alarm clock for months now.

You know what they say: *The early bird gets the worm.* And we get all the sound effects.

However, if high-pitched squeals and low-pitched moans aren't your thing, you're in luck. There is more ruckus in store for you.

Have you ever wanted to visit the African savanna to feel connected to the wildlife there? Run with the giraffes, pet the lions, ride an elephant? While you're going to have to find your own ticket and professional guide to said savanna, why even bother when you're able to experience the magic of elephants *right in your own home*?

Stop wasting time hunting for the best airline deal, and come on over in the morning. Thrills await you.

Imagine: You're camping in a tent on that savanna, snug as a bug with dawn *just* passing the limelight to its cousin, morning. The sun's rays tickle your closed eyes, and all is well as you nestle soundly in your blankets.

Suddenly, your eyes spring open. Your skin decorates itself in goosebumps. The hairs on the back of your neck wake up and stand up, and the rest of you follows.

Oh, no, you realize. A stampede! It's that herd of elephants you saw on the savanna's horizon from last night! How did they get so close? Why is your nest of warmth shaking violently?

Not to fear, dear adventurer. Remember, this is what you signed up for. A morning greeting by your local elephant, as part of your savanna stay. So what if the building tenants are deep into their REM cycle? The rickety wooden stairs right outside your bedroom window *must* be bounded down with great fervor and flourish. A key requirement of this morning stampede is not only must it be heard, but it must be felt. Because you live in California, you must have daily earthquake drills by experiencing the shaking yourself. And what an *honor* to have your neighbor Brian (or is it Bill?) do it for you. *So thoughtful!*

It really doesn't get better than this.

Except it does, for you live in the portly, pink building with three other apartments.

Having three sets of neighbors is quite a joy, because you become a little unit of a community, in part due to how your building is constructed. Remember the building is a giant brick. Part of its charm is it also represents a giant, rectangular bagel, because there is a square opening right in the center.

The opening is loosely reminiscent of an enclosed courtyard, a place for building residents to congregate and relax. However, this opening is tiny, only about three feet by three feet, and does not allow for us neighbors to all come together—not directly, at least.

Sunlight only hits the insides of that opening for a few minutes each day, but that's quite all right, since what you hear makes up for what you *can't* observe.

See, this is where the bathroom windows of all four units converge. While I initially thought the cut-out centerpiece was eccentric, I learned it was an intentional architectural choice. Because this neighborhood was erected in the 1920s, homes lacked a ventilation system.

Prudently, architects decided to put windows in the rooms with the most... fumes, and instead of those windows facing the street, they opened into the hole of this rectangular bagel. In my partner's words, this was the built-in, communal poop chute.

Our bathroom window directly faces that of our upstairs neighbors, and the two units downstairs also face to kiss each other. Every day, there is a make-out session of sounds that get amplified in the tunnel-like column, emanating from and drifting into each of the four openings.

"Goddammit, ow! Fuckin' ingrown toenail!" My own toes curl under in empathy when I hear one neighbor's yelp, accentuated by dry sounds of *clip, clip, clip*. My heart goes out to him in knowing pain.

Other times, I'm transported to the other side of the country without having to get up from the (toilet) seat. A light flickers on across the way, and from the frosted window I can't see into. Thankfully, a sharp sound pierces the silence. *Ahh, the grand fury of Niagara Falls!*

Living in this complex never fails to astound me, especially as it concerns the functions of the human body. I never knew a bladder could hold that much and expel it with such force, such gusto! Sometimes, our neighbors' sounds produce a much-needed mask for what comes out of our own echoey chamber.

In fact, when the neighbors aren't having a party between the bedsheets or stomping on stairs to ensure we're awake, they are extraordinarily supportive. Rarely have I felt so seen and heard and held in moments so intimate.

Imagine: our first Monday living here after the weekend move. It's early. Coffee's brewing. I'm mentally psyching myself up for work where I'm "on" the entire day, facilitating virtual learning experiences for business leaders.

Typically, I'm a morning person, so my brain starts going as soon as my eyes pop open. This weekday is no different, and I'm a hamster running through the to-do list in my head.

A pause. *Duty calls.*

Grateful, I answer. Ahh, a moment of silence and peace where I can be alone with my thoughts and let it all go.

It's delightfully quiet, and as I'm sitting there, a *brrrp!* escapes.

Nice! That was one of the most satisfying farts in a while.

Suddenly, a voice.

"Bless you!"

Instantly, my face blooms in redness and heat. I want to crawl where no one can see me, but remember no one, indeed, can see me. However, I'd forgotten how well the sounds carry through this holy bathroom congregation.

"Thank you!" I chirp back.

What else is there to do?

"Welcome to the neighborhood!" the voice quips again, immeasurably cheerful.

By now I'm laughing and creating mini earthquakes of mirth and mortification. I thank my lucky stars I have my phone nearby and turn on an upbeat Spotify playlist to mask any subsequent sounds for the remainder of my time in the bathroom.

Later, after guffawing about the experience with my boyfriend, I reflect on how lucky I am, too, to be surrounded by people who bless *my* loud sounds, no matter where they come from.

As with any new life chapter, I had a seed of trepidation about creating a sense of belonging for myself within my community. *Will I fit in? Will my neighbors like me?*

In the months since my partner and I moved into this quirky building, our collective sounds *became* the sounds of community. A warm summer night in the backyard brought about the clinking of beer bottles to celebrate filmmaker Jim's new movie short.

A cooler autumn evening became the backdrop for our raucous voices to share tales of our lives. A shower singalong to The Killers from either Brian or Bill invited me to yell across the window, "You've got great music taste!"

We revel in and share our sounds.

One recent morning as I was walking downstairs to the backyard, my neighbor Chris waved as he watered his garden.

"Hey, Katya!" he said with a devilish grin. "Was that you two or the cats we heard rumbling around last night?"

Blushing, I lied, "Oh, you know how our cats get, running up and down the hallway past midnight!"

Chris smirked as I scuttled away, chuckling to myself.

Was he the one who'd blessed my farting sounds all those months ago? What else does he hear?

That will forever remain a mystery.

What is for certain is despite—or thanks to—paper-thin walls and too-close bathrooms, I've come to cherish my neighbors' individual expressions. How lovely is it we get to co-exist in this giant brick of a building, with our farts and our grunts and our unique cacophony of life domestic.

It really doesn't get better than this.

LAUGHTER YOGA

—

"Congrats! You all just laughed for twenty minutes, and we didn't even tell a joke!"

The Laughing Lovebugs, as they were so aptly named, gave us a round of applause from their little rectangle on the Zoom screen, and I saw their wide smiles reflected in the faces of my coworkers. We all chuckled in unison.

For a whole hour one Friday morning, Lauren and Alik, a real-life couple and certified laughter yogis, remotely guided participants at my company through a series of intentional laughing, breathing, and meditative exercises.

First, we started with some *ho ho ho*s, followed by *hee hee hee*s, and dove right into *ha ha ha*s.

This was indeed a real, work-sponsored event, and I had been looking forward to laughter yoga all week.

Now, if you're like most people, you might think, *What sort of millennial nonsense is this? Especially in a professional setting?*

And, I hear you. We, as participants, logged into the Zoom meeting with hints of skepticism and uncertainty etched on our faces.

How could mere pixels on our screen make full-grown adults giggle like children?

Sitting in our individual living rooms or bedrooms in the era of remote work, we would soon be chittering into the void. The only other sound was the collective chorus of chortles emanating from our laptop speakers.

Let me tell you: Laughter yoga is no joke. We got serious about the practice of laughing.

At the beginning of the session, Lauren and Alik set the stage that we may experience some internal resistance. After all, how often do we shed our defenses and laugh—just for the sake of laughing?

Naturally, I dove headfirst into that resistance right away. Even though no one was in my living room besides my cats looking at me in wide-eyed curiosity, a few thoughts raced through my mind as I exhaled *ha ha ha* and *hee hee hee*.

Oh man, am I even laughing correctly? Maybe I should laugh quieter so my colleagues don't hear how weird I sound.

A build-up of tension from the previous week had hiked my shoulders up to my ears. Yet, after the first five minutes of cautious laughter, I noticed my upper body felt warm, fluid.

Hmm, interesting. Some of the tightly wound coils inside began to unravel.

As the group kept laughing in response to Lauren and Alik's various prompts and ending them by clapping and chorusing, "Very good, very good, yay!" I began paying more attention to the chortles of some of my work friends. One had such a jolly high-pitched giggle it made me shake with laughter even harder. Another had a deep, resonant inhale that sounded like an oboe, which the other participants and I found side-splitting. We shed tears of laughter together.

Even the cheesiness of repeating "Very good, very good, yay!" seemed to lose its lactose. I clapped louder with glee as the hour went on.

Looking back, even though I was known as the smiley, optimistic, and easy-to-laugh one by childhood friends, I grew up in a household where perfection was demanded and messing up merited punishment.

Accidentally spill something on the floor? *Get ready for loud berating.*

Bed not made to five-star hotel standards? *Strip the covers and do it again.*

Get into a near-fatal car crash? *Have the first phrase out of your father's mouth on the phone be "Is the car okay?"*

I did find quite a bit of laughter with one parent but came to expect harsh criticism from the other. Laughter was not the norm half the time in our household.

As a kid, I'd learned to laugh at things that were deemed funny, like books, movies, or jokes, and to treat life seriously otherwise. Perhaps in part due to our work-hard-always immigrant mentality—or just the sternness and rigidity of my father's parenting style—I only recall a handful of instances when we all laughed to tears as a family.

When I started living on my own in college, imagine the unlearning I so desperately needed to do.

A few weeks ago, my partner and I spent an entire Saturday afternoon bustling around in the kitchen. We brined and roasted chicken, spiced pan-roasted vegetables to perfection, and crafted a colorful salad to complete the meal. After hours of work, Nick and I grabbed the utensils to serve ourselves, when suddenly, he dropped his plate piled high with food.

A large portion of what we'd worked so hard to make was now laying in a splattered mess on the kitchen floor.

I remember thinking two things in that moment: one, just how furiously I'd get yelled at if this happened to me as a kid; and two, I had a choice.

I had a choice to laugh about this *oopsie-daisy*, and so, grabbing a handful of paper towels from the counter, laugh I did.

As Nick and I wiped up the last of the mess, I smiled at him and said, "If only we'd grabbed some Butterfingers for dessert!"

Back on the Zoom screen, at the end of laughter yoga, Laughing Lovebugs Lauren and Alik shared with us the beauty and benefits of cackling like there's no tomorrow.

Traditionally, they said, our modern society tends to laugh in certain conditions. First, we might laugh when things are genuinely funny, like a dad joke, a pet tripping over itself trying to chase a toy, or a surprise fart. Then, we laugh in *learned* conditions: We may chuckle half-heartedly or otherwise risk unnecessary coldness when a corporate executive makes a "funny" "joke" to stroke their ego, or join a group guffaw to make fun of something or someone to be considered part of the in-crowd.

But there is a third category: laughing for the sake of laughter. It's the ability of those effervescent individuals who light up a room with their guffaws and bring joy and levity to a situation, even when we least expect it.

Those people *choose* to laugh.

Part of what the laughter experts taught us is we don't have to logic ourselves into laughing in specific situations. Instead, we can live and laugh *un*conditionally—that is, without preconceived conditions—by getting comfortable with the uncomfortable.

I thought about all the trepidation, hints of anxiety, and even self-judgment I felt at the beginning of laughter yoga. I was fully in a state of discomfort, both physically and mentally.

But even in that situation—and in other conditions laced with stress and anxiety—we still have the ability to make the lighthearted choice. We can choose how we process and navigate our emotions that arise.

Drop a mug and it shatters? *Hoopla! Why not try a chuckle?*

Fall over and scrape your knee? *Look at you, the prime expert in gravity!*

Create a sonic boom with a sneeze from nowhere? *Hilarious!*

At least that's what a child would think about their own sneeze. Children take moments that adults may think are remarkably unfunny, and react in belly-splitting ways, as if the whole world is set to entertain them.

Perhaps to them, it is.

If we were to put some numbers on it, little kids laugh around three hundred times per day (Gerloff 2011).

These toddlers don't wait for the perfect or "right" moment to break out into giggles; they just *do*. To them, the world is so full of joy and delight, and they sure know how to laugh about it.

Us adults? We laugh as few as four times a day.

Can you remember the last time you had a breathtaking, ab-workout laugh?

Why have we forgotten what it's like to ride the waves of iridescent childhood, smiles plastered on our faces? To let go of that fear and trepidation and self-judgment?

Maybe it's because the world feels heavy. Maybe we have a difficult job, a long commute, demanding family members, an unbearable amount of responsibility. Maybe we navigate our routines with a sense of numbness, or dullness, or exhaustion, with just barely enough energy to put one foot in front of the other.

At the same time, as adults, we get better at logical reasoning, at predicting outcomes or feelings, at building our resilience to the unexpected swings of life's ballgame.

And yet, maybe we pay a price for all our big-brained thinking by forgetting to lighten up. Maybe we have forgotten the art of play.

The other day I was taking my daily neighborhood stroll down the tree-lined streets and spotted some chalk drawings up ahead. Walking closer, I paused to investigate, wracking my brain for what the grid of squares was called, since "hopscotch" was no longer a common word in my vernacular.

Then, I took a jump. And another and another until I got through all the little squares, all the way to ten.

After, I continued my walk with a pep in my step and a huge grin on my face. For the few subsequent weeks that grid had been drawn and recreated—by talented neighborhood children, no less—I'd never seen any adult hop through it.

Just like we may feel trepidation, or embarrassment, or fear of judgment from others for being a huge, gangly human thundering through a self-led game of hopscotch, we, too, have a choice to find the joy and play in it.

What's the worst that could happen?

Maybe you'll bring a shy smile to a stranger's face. Maybe you'll inspire your neighbor to hop *their* own way down the sidewalk. And just maybe, you may choose to see the world through a more vibrant, child-like lens, giggling as you bounce on the hard cement.

And you keep choosing that practice—your own laughter yoga—each moment you get.

Recently at the beach, I saw a dad and his four-year-old daughter walking by the shore, holding hands. Clad in messy blond curls and bubbly smiles, she squealed in sheer joy as the waves from high tide washed up to meet her feet. Without pause, she let go of her dad's hand and began hopping and skipping each time the water kissed her toes, waltzing through the air and sand as if buoyed by the ocean.

Her father watched her for a few seconds and hesitated.

Should he risk looking "silly," this gangly adult human thundering through the sea?

Suddenly, he swung his arms back and jumped into the shallow water, splashing his daughter. Peals of mirth arose from them both.

Their ineffable energy immediately broke my face out into a smile as warmth from witnessing this precious moment spread through my limbs.

Here were two kids, one in an adult body, enjoying themselves so full-heartedly, without a care, the world fully their oyster.

Watching them do their own version of laughter yoga, their own version of play, made me think of a quote by Michael Pritchard:

"You don't stop laughing because you grow old; you grow old because you stop laughing."

And so, I think I'll continue hee-heeing and ha-haing my way through adulthood—whenever that is.

Won't you join me?

LOS LAVADEROS: THE LAUNDROMAT

———

It was a balmy July night. Not the kind where the heat is an oppressive blanket trapping you under a parachute of summer, but one that feels like a hug from your favorite sweater.

My friend Morgan and I were ambling down Sunset Boulevard after a scrumptious dinner of mouth-watering tacos, quesadillas, and fries from a street stand. Over our feast at the plastic-tablecloth-lined tables, we chatted about building a community in Los Angeles and how challenging it was to make friends during the pandemic.

"I don't know, it still doesn't really feel like I'm completely rooted here," I admitted. Both of us had moved to LA within one year of each other—her for grad school, me for a new city.

We were both from a tight-knit town in Virginia, where we met and spent our mid-twenties attending concerts, hikes, coffee dates, and brewery nights together. That town was the closest I'd felt to a sense of belonging, a sense of home.

Relocating to Los Angeles, the second-largest city in the US, forced us to redefine what "home" meant.

One of the things we both appreciated about LA was its hodgepodge of people, cultures, and cuisines. Even this small taco stand contained multitudes. While we were devouring our combination of cheese, bread, and potatoes, Morgan's tiny, black dog, Poco, stole a few fries from the table. I thought about how the respective backgrounds of our dinner trio, two humans and a canine, reflected parts of our meal.

Morgan and I are American, while Poco is from Tijuana, rescued and happy as a clam—or rather as a puppy—under Morgan's care. Coincidentally, we'd both ordered Mexican staples to eat, and all three of us, including Poco, shared the goodness of the quintessential American fried potatoes.

"Mm, I love how you can find literally *any* cuisine in LA," Morgan mused.

"Yeah, especially in this neighborhood. It's such a medley of tastes."

On the way back to her apartment, we walked past a park teeming with children and patient parents. Squeals of happiness provided a pleasant aural background to offset the distant traffic river on the 101. I wondered whether the kids had all grown up here, converging from multiple streets to meet on this very block, every evening at half past six, to play endlessly and build memories they would recall fondly in their later years.

How nice. A true community.

We turned the corner onto Virgil to continue our stroll, discussing the merits of empathy in the workplace, to complement our prior conversations about building meaningful connections with other humans. In this part of town, the main thoroughfare, Virgil Avenue, housed old and gentrified apartment buildings, mom-and-pop shops mixed with local but fancy bars, and an assortment of details to catch our eyes and ears.

After passing an empty parking lot, we came to a prominent green building with the front door open wide. Right as we walked by, we noticed a sleek black cat sitting on the doorstep taking stock of his little sidewalk kingdom.

"Aww, Morgan, look at him!" I couldn't contain my excitement.

There was something about his vibrant emerald eyes that made Morgan and me stop in our tracks and bend down to pet the little creature. As I stuck my hand close to its face, the kitty nudged its nose toward me and began rubbing up on my arm.

Not thirty seconds later, an elderly man, probably in his late sixties, appeared at the door, smiling.

"That's Angelo. He's very friendly."

Morgan and I voiced our agreement as Angelo continued to wrap around our legs. Even Poco was curious and gave her new feline friend a hearty sniffing.

"How old is Angelo?" I inquired.

"Oh, about eight. I got him some time after my wife died to keep me company here."

Here was the green-walled laundromat, with rows of shiny, white washers and dryers lining the walls. Indeed, as I looked at the facade of the building, I saw "Los Lavaderos" in bulky letters.

This block on Virgil Ave housed a significant Hispanic population, and a public laundromat was one of the key buildings on this street to serve anyone and everyone who came through its doors. Interestingly, this coin laundry was part of a chain of Los Lavaderos scattered throughout Los Angeles, but there was something so homey about this particular building and its owner.

The gentleman, still donning his smile, seemed overjoyed we stopped to pet his cat. Looking up at his gray-brown eyes, cataracts seeping in, I immediately felt a sense of warmth, like this man could be my grandfather. We continued to make small talk while I scratched behind the kitty's ears, and the man shuffled back into the laundromat.

"Wait here. I'll be right back," he told us.

Ten seconds later, he came back carrying a cloud.

It was a fluffy, white-orange cat with the most beautiful, deep blue eyes and a feather of a tail. He placed her down next to us, next to Angelo, and I reached out my fingers to make her acquaintance. She sniffed reluctantly, and ran back into the laundromat.

"Ah, yeah, she is shy," the man said.

I smiled at the contrast between the two feline dwellers: a black, sleek one, patrolling the grounds, and his opposite, a downy, light-catching ball of fuzz keeping the laundry machines company. It seemed like a match made in heaven.

I thought, too, about the match this gentleman must have been with his late wife. While his business housed curious cats and laundry machines, his wrinkle-lined eyes housed the rare type of kindness that seemed to accompany a difficult past. They contained the type of warmth inspired by a genuine desire to connect with people of all kinds, both friends and strangers alike.

As I pet Angelo with hypnotic strokes down the ridge of his back, I melted into a brief daydream. *What could this man's life have been like? What led him here, to this laundromat and his two cats? What made his and his wife's eyes shine?*

I let my mind wander to envision this one stranger's life.

I imagined them meeting in grade school in Mexico, a spunky, sassy girl teasing the almost painfully shy boy. I heard the sprinkle of her laugh, the gentle invitation of his voice telling her *ven aquí*. Something about his eyes magnetized her, and they spent their teenage years reveling in each other, discovering parts of themselves only as lovers can.

In their early twenties, fueled by indefatigable lust, they snuck from Tijuana first to San Diego, then up the coast to the City of Angels. They had heard this bustling American city was the land of opportunities, the land of the stars, the land of miracles.

Things were far from easy those first few years. Every month, they struggled to make ends meet as he bounced from service job to service job, and she made meager money as a tailor's assistant. They were poor, homesick, and longed for the lively nights of their childhood, surrounded by friends and what small families they had, coming together to share a communal meal and dance boisterously.

I imagined Maribel grew up with a single mother and a father she'd never met. Matías' mother died when he was just four years old, and he couldn't really get close to his father, their ideas and fists often at odds because the patriarch was steeped in macho culture. However, their small *barrio*, with friends, distant cousins, and the neighborhood children, provided the support and livelihood they so craved.

After their first four years in LA, a letter showed up in the mailbox of their tiny, near-rundown apartment right off Virgil Ave. It was Maribel's cousin writing her mother had died.

She collapsed into Matías as the letter collapsed to the floor. With the flood of tears came the piercing stab of loneliness, the realization it was just them now, alone in California, alone in the world. They still felt isolated in their neighborhood, both too American for the local Mexicans and too Mexican for the Americans. On long walks through the city, they would gaze upward, spying the scant visible stars, and make wishes, hoping for a miracle.

And a miracle did come. Through a serendipitous break, Matías had gotten in as the night shift clerk at the twenty-four-hour laundromat down the street. It was a relatively easy gig, and quiet, too, giving him time to observe the habits of the regulars.

On the fourth night, it was just him and one other man in his forties finishing up a load.

"*¿Oíste éso?*" Matías asked the man, pointing to his ear.

The man looked at him, squinted his eyes and cocked his head in concentration, listening, and shook his head. "No."

After the man grabbed his clothes from the dryer and made his way toward the exit, Matías followed him out and heard that sound again.

It was a tiny squeak, high-pitched and persistent. He looked around the open door of the laundromat and in the murky velvet of night, saw...nothing.

Matías shuffled around the area, squatting down left and right to try to follow the noise. The squeaks grew more determined, and then, something caught his eye.

Two little orbs flickering at certain angles beckoned him closer, and he followed the light to the parking lot next to his building. At the corner by the gate, he saw a tiny orange kitten.

When Matías approached it gently, it hissed in fear at first. Pausing and hitching his breath, he switched strategies and made a *pspspsps* sound with his lips, and the kitten answered in meows that sounded like question marks.

Matías bent down slowly and reached out his hands to gingerly scoop up the warm, tiny body. Curiously, the kitten didn't try to fight or run away. It was as if something was magnetizing one to the other.

"*Ven aquí*," Matías cooed to him.

Back inside his laundromat, he grabbed a basket and a pile of discarded clothes someone had forgotten for the past week. He gently placed the kitten in the nest of shirts and socks and counted down the minutes until his night shift was over.

That morning, Matías bounded into their bedroom, where Maribel was still in the throes of what seemed like a nightmare. She hadn't been sleeping well the last few weeks ever since the news about her mother.

"¡*Mira*, Maribel!"

Matías' excitement bubbled over as he held the orange furball next to his lover's face. She scrunched up her nose and opened one eye, squinting, and sat up with a jolt.

"*¿Un gatito?*" she exclaimed.

The kitten, now on the bed, bravely walked up to her body under the blankets, and climbed onto her chest. There, he plopped down between the valley of her nightgown, and began to purr.

"Let's name him *Milagro*. *Él es nuestro miracle*."

Matías and Maribel smiled at each other, sensing their little miracle was a sign of good things to come.

And the following year was indeed a harbinger of good. The owner of Los Lavaderos, José, promoted Matías to run the day shift, so now the couple spent their evenings playing with Milagro and continuing their long walks. They even tried taking the cat on strolls around the block, which he surprisingly, if not gladly, accompanied them on.

Of course, seeing a couple ambling down the streets of LA with an orange tabby in tow was not a common sight, so the three of them attracted quite a bit of attention. Little kids stopped to pet Milagro, and Matías and Maribel were able to get to know their fellow neighbors bit by bit. Their English improved significantly. Their smiles grew wider. Their hearts ached less for Tijuana.

And then, another year down the line, José called Matías into the little back office one day in the spring.

"Listen, Matías, I'm not getting any younger. I see how hard you work here, keeping it clean and running. I see how you engage with customers—regulars and newcomers alike. Washing clothes ain't glamorous, but somehow you make people smile while they do it."

"I've been running Los Lavaderos for over forty years. My wife's health is declining, and I need to go be with her and make the best of our remaining time and my remaining years. I want you to take over my business."

Matías was stunned. Here was a miracle staring directly into his eyes. He would be a business owner! He could hardly believe it! Just last month, he and Maribel got their paperwork approved to become American citizens. Now, he was really living the dream among the stars. His community back in Tijuana would be so proud.

"José, *gracias*! I would be honored. I promise I won't let you down."

And so Matías became the owner of Los Lavaderos. He began bringing his little Milagro to work to keep him company. Interestingly, he found when the cat was around, the customers seemed to laugh more and share bits of their lives with him while folding freshly dried clothes.

He'd heard about one young man's plan to propose to his girlfriend, another *abuelita* delighted by her tenth grandchild, a single mom fearful about affording her son's soccer team dues. Each joy and each sorrow moved Matías deeply and he came home every night to retell the tales of his customers to Maribel.

By that time, they'd been trying to create a little joy of their own, but after one unsuccessful attempt after another, they'd learned she couldn't have children. Disheartened, Matías withdrew into his work running the laundromat, and Maribel would cry at night, cuddling Milagro for comfort.

During the day, if Matías was out running an errand, she would often find herself at Los Lavaderos, in the company of both her cat and the strangers whose stories Matías wove over the last several years. She was most drawn to the children who accompanied their mothers and fathers, who, in turn, were drawn to Milagro. They would tickle him, give him cuddles and pets, and sometimes bring him a piece of chicken from the taco stand down the street. He reveled in their attention, and she reveled in the levity they brought to the laundromat.

Because she couldn't have kids, Maribel decided to channel her energy into cultivating kids' minds instead. She took night classes at the local community college just a few blocks down from the laundromat and applied for her teaching license.

The week she found out she would be teaching fourth grade English in the fall, Matías put up banners and balloons in Los Lavaderos to celebrate her and share the happiness with the community. Curious, folks passing by the forest-green laundromat stepped inside to ask about the decorations and were greeted by Matías' wide smile and his orange cat.

"My wife is a teacher!" he beamed, holding Milagro in his arms.

"We have a business and careers and this cat!"

Over the years, the laundromat became a staple on Virgil Ave, while Maribel became a staple in the classroom. The students loved her, and Matías would often see them and their parents wash and fold their laundry in his laundromat. On their beloved evening walks, kids and adults alike would wave to them, call out hellos, and ask about Milagro.

Matías and Maribel finally felt they'd found their community. Life was good.

And it continued to be good. For over two and a half decades, Matías' business boomed as more people moved to their neighborhood, and Maribel won several teaching awards because of her dedication and care for every single student. After Milagro passed, a whopping twenty-two years after that first meow in the parking lot, Matías began leaving saucers with tuna outside the laundromat door for the strays. Some he'd only see at night, as he was finishing his shift, and others would wander shyly into the building, only to run out when he tried to approach them, *pspspsps*-ing, hand outstretched.

They had their cats, their patrons, their students, their neighbors, their friends. It was exactly the community they'd dreamed of. Their life, centered around Virgil Avenue, became a home so much warmer, so much more rooted, than they could have ever imagined.

Then, Maribel became ill.

It wasn't a sudden onset, but more of a gradual, increased feeling of fatigue. The couple thought it was due to some particularly challenging students that year, or maybe all the smog in Los Angeles had finally gotten to her.

Maribel kept trying to quell Matías' persistent insistence to visit the doctor.

"*Ay, querido*, it's okay, I'm fine, I'm okay. Just a little tired, that's all."

But when her students started asking why she'd gotten so skinny or why she started teaching them the same lesson as yesterday, Maribel booked an appointment at the clinic.

In the sterile white room, a bitter memory surfaced from deep in her bones. It was that same feeling, as if a vacuum stole all the air from around her, that same taste of death.

Stage four breast cancer. Terminal.

Just like her mother.

The doctors gave her two months to live.

She held on for nine weeks. Matías fell apart, sobbing with heart-wrenching heaves, at her last words.

"Take care of yourself, Matías. Take care of the *gatitos*. You still have a home, a community without me. Don't mourn me. Remember the light."

The months after the service felt like he was the one six feet under. He was a walking ghost, robotically going to work and coming straight home to sit in bed until sleep consumed him. No more evening walks, no more conversations with neighborhood friends. He only made sure to feed the strays every day; he couldn't bear to see another living thing die.

As the years passed, the waves of grief pummeled him from time to time. It's not it hurt less; he'd just built a more fortified boat. Often, the only things that kept him going were the tabbies at Los Lavaderos and his duty to his community on Virgil Avenue. At least the tides in the washing machines were contained.

Nearly two decades after Maribel's passing, Matías still hadn't remarried. He kept a picture of her hanging on the western wall of the laundromat, so her face, her memory, would be ignited in fiery sunrise streaming through the windows every morning.

Many of his patrons now wore familiar faces with early etchings of crow's feet and laugh lines. Some were Maribel's students, all grown up, who stayed in their childhood hometown and visited Matías every few weeks. As they folded their laundry, they'd tell him stories of what she was like in the classroom: her animated laugh that got all students giggling in unison, her infectious energy that brought the tales from books they read to life.

And in a way, these memories brought Maribel back to life for Matías, if only for a few moments. They made him feel more embedded within their rich history and more connected to his love. On occasion, one of the former students would bring in *her* own children, who'd immediately be magnetized to his cats, stroking them and throwing balls of lint for the rambunctious felines to chase.

Every few days, those kids would stop by on the way home from school or en route to the playground to feed and pet the strays. Seeing those little kids, with such pure joy and squeals of delight when the kittens would paw at their tiny fingers, bubbled up a warm affection and comfort in his heart. Oh, how Maribel would have loved to witness this!

And Matías did his best to keep her spirit alive. He shared all the joy and delight his little community provided, especially with any inquiring passersby.

On that particular balmy July evening, Morgan, her puppy Poco, and I were those inquiring passersby, drawn to the warmth of the man running the forest-green laundromat on Virgil Ave.

As the daydream of this one stranger's life faded, the black cat at my feet came back into focus. Angelo had, by this point, melted into my hands, purring and rubbing his head intently as I continued stroking his whiskered face. Here was a cat who felt right at home with strangers, who so easily created a microcosm of unity amid the bustle of the street.

And even though that wasn't my neighborhood, I felt welcomed. This could very well have been *my* laundromat, *my* street peppered with footprints of friends and neighbors, *my* little melting pot of a community. I observed how easily Poco played with Angelo, finding boundless joy in a cross-species mate, while we humans from different worldly corners meshed in casual conversation.

Perhaps that was what a sliver of "home" in Los Angeles felt like. Maybe it was the lanes of our lives converging for a few miles on the freeway, only to peel off for the next interaction. Fleeting in time, lasting in memory.

Over time, these tiny moments of connection weave into a feeling of rootedness. *This* is where I get my taste of Mexico. *This* is where I grab my morning coffee. *This* is where I wash my clothes.

I thought about the little mountain town in Virginia Morgan and I called home. How I was a Tuesday regular at my favorite brewery whose beer and community were only available locally. How I could walk into my favorite, one-of-a-kind coffee shop and melt into the seat and my work, only to be punctuated by short but meaningful conversations with strangers and friends alike. How I could bound down the steps of my red house on my sloped street, and in the ten minutes it took to walk to downtown, I'd wave hello to ten people who were *my people.*

All these places, rooted in light conversations with strangers we see as part of our routines, bits of our past histories rising to weave a cohesive blanket of *us* and *we* and *community.*

A blanket of home, much like that hug from your favorite sweater.

Two years and a pandemic later, I still don't really have that in Los Angeles. Sure, I walk to my local Starbucks and the watering hole down the street and exchange jokes in the garden with my neighbors. Sure, I've turned a stranger into a good friend by sharing a chat at a non-chain coffee shop, but that's an exception, not the rule.

LA's hugs are brief, uneasy.

Maybe that's why I'm drawn to places like the green laundromat. This tiny speck on Virgil Ave draws in long-time residents, new arrivals, and unsuspecting passersby to pause and share a moment of community with an old man and his cat.

Who knows if Matías' story was true. Who knows if he had a Maribel, a Milagro, and the colorful past my mind dreamt up.

What mattered was the kindness this elderly man extended to us, warmth emanating from his cloudy eyes, where inside, a little boy squealed with delight at the chance to share words and feline love with strangers.

We gave Angelo one final round of scratches, and I thanked the owner of Los Lavaderos for letting us revel in this moment. In return, he asked where Poco was from.

"I got her from Tijuana," Morgan said.

He smiled, with a twinkle of familiarity in his eye: a home in many places.

His was the light I remembered.

AN ODE TO ALDI

"Mom, you don't need another candle!"

An exasperated cry came from a teenager stuck on a grocery run with his mother late one Thursday night. The three of us were in the "goods" aisle, not to be confused with the edible "goodies" aisle a few feet over.

All around us were towering shelves of alarm clocks, food tongs and other kitchen accessories, blow-up pool rafts and toys. It was the sneaky type of aisle that could convince you that you *definitely* needed the item that somehow ended up in your hands.

The mom just smiled at her son and picked up another jewel-colored jar, lifted the lid, and inhaled through her mask. The son rolled his eyes, smirking, and left to wander in the goodies section.

I, too, was in the candle area, slapping my own metaphorical hands away from adding to my collection.

"You know," I said smiling, turning to the lady, "you can never really have too many candles."

She glanced up and crinkled the corners of her eyes, revealing a smile that seemed to emanate even beyond the boundaries of her mask.

"Right?" she exclaimed. "They just make the home so much cozier."

"I hear you! I'm having to stop myself from buying more. Last time I was here, I got a lemon-and-sage one. And before that, something peachy. What scent do you have there?"

"It's pumpkin spice, perfect for the season!"

I eyed a row of orange jars on the shelf in front of me and picked one up to inhale.

Eyes running wild at the selection, I exclaimed cheerfully, "Mmm, there's even a chocolate-chip cookie-scented one here!"

The lady found the matching beige candles near her section of shelving and opened the jar to take in the aroma.

"The only problem with these candles is I always crave cookies when the house smells like them. It can be a dangerous game," I said.

The mom locked eyes with mine and nodded enthusiastically.

"Oh totally. I think I'm going to get this juniper one here. My daughter likes more masculine scents."

I didn't question how juniper was a manly aroma and bid her a lovely rest of her evening.

She smiled back with a "You too, honey!"

We parted ways, and I maneuvered my heavy cart to the only operating checkout line. As I was about to begin unloading, I saw a woman around my age get in line behind me holding just two items. I backed out my cart from the tight aisle and told her she could check out first.

"You've got two things. I have a whole cart. Go ahead, I'm in no rush." Another chance to share a kindness with a masked stranger.

She smiled gratefully, pausing to ask if I was sure, and stepped in front of me.

As I waited my turn, my eyes caught the array of gum, and I threw an off-brand container of spearmint cubes into the cart. It seemed like a fair tradeoff for resisting a candle purchase this time. A rewarding trip to the grocery store indeed.

I'm not exactly sure when my love affair with Aldi began. Growing up as an immigrant without much money for frivolous spending, I remember being overjoyed when a sunshine-yellow box would show up in our pantry once in a blue moon.

The box contained six pairs of decadent chocolate-covered peanut butter wafers, encased in thin, clear plastic. After gingerly opening the wrapper, I would meticulously peel the layers apart, scrape the peanut butter off with my teeth, and munch on the satisfying crunch of the crispy wafer. It was a learned art of making the good things last.

Since we lived in the suburbs of Washington, DC, with access to plenty of grocery stores, my parents would make the hour-long trek to buy Aldi-specific goodies only a few times a year. However, I distinctly recall the days and weeks *after* they unloaded Aldi's groceries from several boxes in the trunk as some of the richest and tastiest days of my childhood.

They'd stock up on canned evaporated milk to put in their coffee, a whole pallet of sweetened condensed milk, also for coffee but mostly to eat right off the spoon, and other sweets we all longed for when it wasn't Aldi season.

It was a time of bounty. Memories associated with Aldi were tinged with sweetness—and were a stark contrast to how I grew up in Uzbekistan.

After the fall of the Soviet Union, a time of lack became the norm. When I was around five or six years old, I distinctly recall standing in line with my mother, waiting—hoping—for a loaf of bread. The line stretched out the store door and spilled onto the street, probably forty to fifty people deep, each adult anxiously thinking, *I hope there's some left for my family.*

Inevitably, when the stock would run out, an outcry of anger and fright would resonate through the dirty streets. Every week, some of us went hungry.

Other times, as my mother would share with me years later, butchers would put pebbles on the scale when weighing out meat to swindle customers into paying more than what the bone-filled chunk was worth. And yet, there was nothing anyone could do against the corruption.

Except flee.

When we came to the States, I felt like Charlie walking through Willy Wonka's chocolate factory. My eyes were saucers at the sheer selection of goods readily available for purchase, sans any hidden agendas, political or otherwise.

Accordingly, stepping into my first Aldi at around nine years old, aisles filled to the sky with goodies, was a goddamn miracle. The frenetic energy of people clamoring for life-sustaining food from my past was now replaced with friendly Americans making difficult choices between red or green peppers. How far we'd come: from bread lines to bell peppers!

Aldi was an immigrant daughter's dream.

During my senior year of college, a few weeks after surviving a serious car crash, I was deep in the process of interviewing for my first "real" nine-to-five job. One of them happened to be a rotational leadership development program where bright-eyed and bushy-tailed graduates could grow their management skills in a variety of business roles for two years, before choosing a specialized path in corporate.

The company?

Aldi.

I recall nervously getting into the rental car Aldi generously offered, since my own car was totaled, and psyching myself up for a safe trip three hours north. Dressed in an official suit with copies of my resume in a professional portfolio, I drove for the first time since the accident on narrow country roads to Maryland.

During the two-day interview process, which was also paid for, I got to learn how the chain worked and what made them so efficient.

The leaders explained the reason carts cost a quarter to use: to eliminate the reliance on a cart clerk and to incentivize shoppers to return the carts themselves. They articulated why groceries were stored in their original packaging as a way to decrease labor costs of unpacking, similar to Costco's model. Finally, they demonstrated the humanity in their company by making it acceptable and even encouraged for cashiers to sit on a comfortable highchair while checking out and putting groceries into customers' carts.

I didn't end up accepting the offer at Aldi because I wanted to explore beyond the grocery store industry, but the experience amplified my appreciation for them as a company.

After college, while I built up my career in consulting, higher education, and ultimately organizational development, I looked forward to the days I'd visit my parents and their well-stocked pantry. They'd surprise me with an afternoon snack consisting of coffee creamed with Aldi's evaporated milk and those famous peanut butter wafers from the yellow box. Those treats, while objectively bad for health, were a balm for the soul; they brought me so much joy and memories of a sweet time.

When I moved across the country to Los Angeles half a decade later, I had to acclimate to the world of Ralph's, Von's, and bougie boutique grocery stores that sold a pint of cherry tomatoes for fifteen dollars a pop. While I did most of my shopping at my neighborhood chain grocery store, I longed for the familiar aisles, for the same feeling of wonder and bounty I had at nine years old. I wondered whether California had an Aldi in my vicinity.

Luckily, it did!

There was a brand-new store opening in Burbank, only seventeen minutes away. I was thrilled.

I texted my father with the news, since he was also a huge fan of the store and the primary buyer of those peanut butter wafers of my childhood. With his "hoorah!" I set out on my first Aldi run.

Grocery shopping as an adult is the *utmost* fun. While many people view it as a chore, I *love* going up and down the aisles, picking from the bounty of vegetables, fruits, and snacks.

Feeling like getting a family-sized bag of chocolate-covered almonds for one? Why not! What about some salty prosciutto to eat straight from the container? Of course!

I think back to little Katya, walking around my first American grocery store dumbfounded, holding my mom's hand and my eyeballs spinning madly. It really seemed like a divine promise land on the opposite end of the spectrum from our days standing in line for moldy bread.

Now, as an adult, I don't think an iota of that magic has worn off. I still marvel at how much we're able to purchase within one warehouse-like building.

A few of my friends also share this sentiment. After my most recent Aldi trip, I chatted with one of my work friends about—you guessed it—Aldi. I asked her if she'd ever been there.

"Katya," she started with a mischievous grin, "of *course* I know Aldi! You know, it's funny. As a kid, I used to think Aldi was actually 'All These,' like *look at 'all these' things you can buy!* So, when my parents got back from their shopping trips, I also marveled at all these new snacks from Aldi."

I grinned at my kindred friend and told her about my own experience with the candle-loving mom.

It's these very stories of human connection at Aldi that keep me coming back. During my first two years in LA, I would go every two or three weeks to stock up. Now I live in the house with the lemon tree further west, the trek to the closest Aldi takes around thirty-five minutes without traffic. And since I live with my partner, we switch grocery duty every two weeks, so my trips to my beloved store happen even less frequently, only once a month.

Even though several stores within a mile are bursting with groceries, I still look forward to those fourth Thursdays around 8 p.m. That's when I walk up to the cart with my quarter in hand, ready to shop, knowing I have a full hour before the store closes.

It's when I meet an Indian woman with henna in her hair, a connection sparked by her affinity to my boots. She notices my gray suede shoes as we both reach for the Roma tomatoes, and I notice the orange glint in her hair.

"This may be a weird question, but do you happen to use henna?" I inquire.

She gives me the widest smile and replies, "How did you know?"

Buoyed by our shared styling choices, we go on to swap stories about how our moms and our grandmothers before them put the dye in our hair to give it a healthy shine and a colored hue.

It's when I chat with a sixty-year-old man and we discover we have similar career interests in making organizations function better and more humanely. We joke about what we want to do when we grow up and bid each other good luck with our respective dreams.

It's when a grandmother and I delight in the price of avocados—*forty-five cents each; can you believe it?* The avocado shortage crisis apparently never existed here at Aldi.

It's when I get out of my car at 7:59 p.m. and realize I completely forgot to bring a quarter for the cart. It's been a whole month, after all. Luckily, the man in the car right next to mine is finishing loading his groceries. I ask if I can take his cart back to the store, and shrugging, he says, "Sure!" Now I have a cart *and* a quarter. What bounty!

At the end of the day, Aldi is just a grocery chain. It has largely the same products as your local store. However, especially during the pandemic when the world shut down, a trip to Aldi was an excursion to the land of the plenty, to the land of smiling, unfamiliar faces, warmth radiating from beneath the masks.

In a noisy world, it transformed a mundane, mindless chore into an hour every few weeks when I could focus. I could be intentional with my time to select healthful, delicious products to nourish myself and my partner, *and* get the benefit of social interaction.

Going to *my* grocery store became the glint of joy in the ordinary. And now, with only two weeks until my next Aldi trip, I'm already planning the shopping haul.

You better believe those peanut butter wafers will be at the top of the list.

DRIVING RICH

———

I don't know about you, but the only time I think about license plate frames is when it's time to change the registration sticker.

Each summer, I log into the clunky DMV website and pay the ludicrous car registration renewal fee. Like magic, a small white envelope shows up in my mailbox a week later, containing the tiny rectangular and reflective flag with the following year's digits.

After a week-long battle with procrastination, I gather all the necessary accoutrements and trudge over to my car. It is time for the changing of the guard—for the little sticker to uproot its temporary residence on the DMV paper and sign a year-long lease for the top-right corner of my license plate. It is quite the formal process indeed.

Screwdriver in hand (although I'm never sure which specific *type* is needed; how do people just *know* the Phillips head from the other one?), I squat down by my car's back bumper and begin the unleashing. I jam the pointy end into the surprisingly shiny nails and twist, whispering to myself, "Lefty loosey, righty tighty." That is perhaps one of the most important phrases in the English language.

I pick out the nails, place them gingerly on the concrete below, and lift the plastic frame. Finally, I slide out the metal plate from its flimsy casing and carefully—with the precision of one of those Boston Dynamics robots—affix the sticker on top of the stack of prior years' stickers. Voilà! Expert-level work right there. The contrast of the little yellow rectangle against the white plate rivals Piet Mondrian's works. *And who says we're not artists?*

Finally, I grab the newly adorned license plate and shove it back into the frame, amused at how clunky it feels. The process reminds me of the friction of the DMV experience, which is fitting, since they mandate this changing of the guard in the first place.

I glance at the frame: "Fairfax Toyota," silver embossed letters on a strip of jet black. Plain and simple, and tells you everything you need to know, which is ultimately nothing more than the city in which the car was purchased. I'd give the marketing department of those frames a solid C-plus with their minimalist, no-frills design.

It makes me think about the frame for approximately 2.7 seconds once each year, and that seems plenty. Nothing more to see here; the job is done.

A few months after my most recent plate adventure, I was walking down a tree-lined street in an affluent neighborhood in Los Angeles. As if the size and column count of the mansions wasn't enough, the cars that paralleled the curbs also screamed, "I'm rich!" I saw Teslas, Audis, Jaguars, and Maseratis, most of which had vanity license plates. Up ahead, I passed by a Beamer with something on the back bumper that caught my eye.

On a plastic rectangle (plastic! Why wouldn't it be made of platinum, for instance?) were the words, "World Famous Beverly Hills BMW."

My interest in this license plate frame skyrocketed. A *world-famous* Beverly Hills car?

The hyperbolic word choice of the BMW marketing department tickled my funny bone. Sure, I get people love their cars. And particularly in a city where brand names speak volumes—more so about their *perceived* societal value—it made me wonder how famous this car's owner actually felt when cruising through the city.

Later that night, fueled by curiosity, I looked up the street view on Google Maps of this so-called "World Famous Beverly Hills BMW." I expected light-up signs and banners galvanizing people to visit.

Instead, across from a vape shop and a one-hour cleaners stood a monolithic gray building, framed by more gray sidewalks. From a bird's eye view, there was a giant, slate-colored parking lot housing an array of tiny cars, all lined up in rows.

This world-famous attraction was a mere car dealership.

Three thousand miles away, I searched for the Fairfax Toyota in my hometown.

The similarities were striking.

Stripping away the brands, the dealerships looked almost identical: hundreds of cars sitting on hundreds of square feet of cement.

And on each of these cars—be they Toyotas or BMWs—sat a flimsy, plastic frame to advertise their origin. All these cars came from a similar place—factories of metal and plastic—assembled in similar ways by robot or human hands. I wondered where these cars would go.

Did their headlights illuminate the same bougie streets, or worse, the insides of a dark garage to protect the fine body work from LA grime? Or did the wheels spin madly across miles of highway infinite as the desires of their driver?

Over the last fifteen years, my own car has seen tremendous adventure—and has the beautiful scars to prove it.

Since my first car was totaled in the wreck during college— also a Toyota, albeit from a different part of Northern Virginia—my parents graciously passed down their second, the "Fairfax Toyota." It was the newer version of our first car, just six years and one boxy design later.

It wasn't fancy, yet it had everything I needed. For a young twenty-something, I was more concerned about where it would take me, rather than what it was made of.

After college graduation, the car carried me to a soul-sucking job every day for one-and-a-half years exactly to the month. I'd inhale a sigh of anxiety in the mornings driving to the pallid corporate office, and exhale a sigh of relief on my way back home. I'd give my car a little pitstop at half past six each night, pausing at my local gym for an hour or two where I could work out my frustrations and make friends by the weight rack.

It was my trusty steed, getting me reliably to my all-too-stable and boring job. Ten miles there, ten miles back, almost in a straight line.

I wondered if it, too, was getting tired of seeing the same suburban streets every day. I sensed it craved more zest.

So, I stuffed my life into the trunk and backseat and set off one hundred miles south, back to my college town for a job that was also stable but slightly less boring. What made these few years colorful were the radiant faces of friends old and new against the backdrop of the rich mahoganies, marmalades, and citrines of the Blue Ridge Mountains in the fall.

In short, my car and I fell in love again with the mountain town I still call home in my heart.

We traveled to the Appalachian Trail, while my car waited patiently as I traipsed up and down single tracks cresting mountain ridges; I wanted to lose sight of those winding tar ribbons. It waited patiently as I lay on a blanket in late autumn, watching sparkles rain down from the inky sky, flames in the trees muted in the night. It carried me constantly from work to breweries to Toastmasters to Kroger to the houses of loved ones, a dizzying era of exploration and fun.

During those two and a half years, too, it steadily made its way up Route 29, all 130 miles, almost every Friday to safely deposit me in my graduate school classes in Washington, DC. Most weekends, my car patiently paralleled the street curb while I absorbed topics about organizational development. Most weekdays, it rested under the shade of the sprawling oak outside my workplace, ready to rumble at any moment.

In that same period of full-time work and a full-time master's and friendships and workouts and loving both cities and their people, my car put on a hefty eighteen thousand miles.

It had housed my mom's home cooking when I stopped by my parents'; it had housed a go-bag of clothes and electronics for any given two-day interval; it had housed grocery receipts and old ticket stubs and the occasional Dunkin' coffee cup; it had housed dates and lovers on the way back from a night out on the town.

It bore witness to wanting bodies, reminiscent of high school lust, pressing noses and foreheads and lips to their succulent counterparts. The car was my own memory box for those years.

While its scope of sights to see and miles to cover expanded greatly, I thought, *What if it wants more?*

And it did.

My car, wizened and dependable, longed for the vastness of the cornfields of the Midwest en route to witnessing the sun setting over the ocean. It longed for an adventure out west.

For the second or twenty-second time—who can really keep track—I shoved my belongings into my trunk and backseat, with my mother as co-pilot, and set off to Los Angeles.

It was the Great American Adventure. Driving from coast to coast, we saw some states color-blocked in the soft, golden shimmer of cornfields contrasted against a sapphire rectangle above. Some were blurry slabs of that same gray cement of car dealership parking lots against an even darker, slate blanket of clouds. Mark Rothko would have been proud of these landscapes.

The vastness of the sky sometimes felt like it could swallow whole us tiny humans in our tiny car and lick its ruby, sunset lips in delight. Steadily, reliably, my car kept gliding westward on the black-and-silver tongue of Mother Earth.

Eight days later, we arrived in Los Angeles.

My car was shocked at the noise. Honks and the screeching of brakes made it feel more aware and also more alive. It had to become more cognizant of its expensive counterparts, be they Teslas, Audis, Jaguars, or Maseratis, especially when they tried to bludgeon its rear bumper or graze its sides. It had to learn to be brave to make a double left-hand turn on red to squeeze through jammed intersections.

Even though it was perpetually hot in its new home, the car still wore a coat of dust and dirt, in part due to my own battle with procrastination. Sometimes, the layer of gray would sit on its body for months on end, until I'd finally had enough and took it to the carwash. I can only imagine the relief my car must have felt after being jostled this way and that with long, rubber appendages, only to emerge the best and brightest version of itself.

It was LA, after all—the land of glitz and glamour.

Through several years of city driving, my car got more and more decorated. A few months after moving, I gifted it a wide turquoise necklace on its rear door after somehow clipping the sea-colored support beam of my apartment's parking structure. While unconventional, I thought it made for a nice contrast against its shimmery, silver body.

Other weeks, a new set of milky scratches would appear on its bumpers even though I tried to park as far away as possible from other cars. I wanted to give it breathing room, space, in a city where there was a million of everything.

Some of those scratches I'd try to buff out, but others were left to their own design. They were little reminders of the furtive, gentle kisses courtesy of others' bumpers.

I suppose my car fell in love with LA, too.

And even though the pandemic lockdowns slashed the places I could go and the miles I could travel, my car remained my steady companion on the occasional excursion. Usually, the humming of tires on potholed asphalt would conclude in a crackling crescendo on a gravel parking lot, somewhere remote in the Angeles National Forest.

It was refreshing to get away from the luxury cars and the gilded feel of LA. Out on the trail, we were unified by the layer of dirt and sweat covering our bodies, tethered to the soil by the consistent crunch of our boots. It didn't matter what kind of vehicle brought us here, be it a Toyota or Tesla.

My car would still sit there for hours, undisturbed, patient, waiting as I clocked five, ten, fifteen miles on the single tracks. Despite taking the freeways to get to the mountains, I felt most free when I could see the roads as microscopic gray lines below.

There, high on mountain tops and fresh air, I couldn't see the traffic, the busyness, or the World Famous Beverly Hills BMW.

What I *could* see were the general directions of where my car had taken me to a sixteen-hour second date with my now-partner at the beach, or the area I'd passed so many times before it became our current home. I saw the neighborhoods with intimate bars and concert venues full of good drinks and better conversations with friends.

All these beautiful memories, thanks to my car getting me there.

And I think the biggest gift this car gave me was depositing me on these very mountaintops, away from the glitz and perceived glamour of the City of Angels.

It gave me the space to think, to weave stories about lemon trees and grocery stores and cats. It took me to solitude. To the time and place for reflection for this very story, for this very book, to be born and adorned with colorful words.

My car is not world-famous. It comes from a nondescript dealership.

But it also goes to places—and takes me with it—that give me the freedom to craft ideas for finding joy in the most mundane rituals, like the yearly changing of the registration sticker. It gives me the freedom to create resplendent memories and piece together jigsawed narratives of the places I've been.

I can only dream of where my trusty car, scars and all, will take me next.

And that feels like driving rich to me.

ON CARRYING THINGS ATOP OUR HEADS

———

Cooler summer evenings draw quite the crowd to Runyon Canyon.

Imagine: a confluence of every shade of human skin, stretched across taut, jiggly, mountainous, miniature bodies of every characteristic in between.

Streaming in and out of the cleavage of Runyon, one has their pick of big-time celebrities (I swear I passed Matthew McConaughey once), celebrity wannabes ("Bro, my TikTok vid got a million views! I'm fuckin' famous, bro!"), and everyone else.

This park is one of the most central recreation areas in Los Angeles, bestowing upon its residents and visitors a swift mountain escape, with sprawling views of the sparkling city below. In a single five-mile loop around the borders of the park, your eyes may flit from the Hollywood Sign, to a soaring hummingbird, to that gargantuan mansion built into the Hollywood Hills themselves, all blocks away from the iconic, eponymous Boulevard marked by tents at every block.

One summer Friday, I found myself huffing and puffing up the steep incline as part of a sweaty workout—not only for my limbs, but for my eyes.

On my left, a gray-and-black mutt trotted happily in front of its owners, an impeccably dressed couple in the finest athleisure. I ran alongside the pup for a few seconds, and called back to the lady, "Your dog is so jolly!"

She smiled, and it was like the light of a thousand suns came pouring out of her perfectly lined ruby lips.

"Thanks! He's such a good boy!" she exclaimed through the straightest, whitest, squarest teeth I'd seen all month in LA. Her cheekbones were meticulously accentuated by bronzer and kissed with blush and highlighter, eyebrow arches styled with sheer precision, and hair carefully coiffed into a gentle swirl at the crown of her head.

For a split second, I questioned whether we were on a dirt path or a runway.

Up ahead, I saw shirtless men with corrugated abs, ladies with tree twigs for legs, and other members of the human race who may only be described as models.

While Runyon Canyon is known as a backdrop for overly saturated Instagram posts with the hashtags #hiking, #blessed, #fitness, #mindbodyandsoul, and #healingvibes, it's not all glamour and glitz. In fact, what draws my eyeballs to linger on specific individuals is not how they look, but how they carry themselves.

At the top of one peak, I stopped to cheer on the woman drawing every last ounce of her energy to summit before I flew down the mountain in her footsteps. There was a cloud of moisture surrounding her, and her face was a mixture of pain and triumph.

"You go, girl!" I cheered.

Later, down that same incline, I became curious about another man in a designer baseball cap in front of me, taking his sweet time. He kept turning around as the distance between us narrowed on the steep single track, sensing I was itching to get past him. Yet he was crawling at a pace slower than molasses in winter. I wondered if he was the type of person who wouldn't let you merge on the freeway.

The man paused at a little clearing with me still hot on his heels and emphatically bent over, hands on knees, panting. I whooshed past him, yelling an unironic "Thanks!" behind me.

Finally, I could make it down the rest of the mountain.

At the bottom, I saw a confluence of shapes and skin tones, all distinct, yet all with one thing in common. Their dainty, meaty, nail-polished, nail-bitten hands all clutched a cylinder of that life-giving liquid. Water.

Some of these water bottles were as bougie as they come: brands that produced only a limited amount each year, others bedazzled by colors and materials unusual for merely a container of H_2O.

After passing dozens of humans carrying themselves in such specific ways over the course of the five-mile loop, I turned my attention to how they carried other things.

Some clutched their plastic as if it was their battery pack; their energy was charging while the bottle was in their hand. Others married their fingers with the bottle's looped handle, sending it for a joy ride 'round and 'round. A few had figured out the best way to carry a water bottle was to not hold it at all, but rather to wear a pouch around the gut or on the back. These were the serious runners, perhaps on their tenth loop around the park.

And through all this reflection on the modes of clutching Earth's most vital resource, an older gentleman caught my eye.

A balding figure in his early sixties was walking up the path to the park with his, presumably, wife. He had white hair, bronze and supple skin, and donned a t-shirt and cargo shorts that looked as if they had withstood years of adventures.

He walked confidently with his back stick straight. I *hmm*-ed to myself, impressed at the man's posture precisely because it was so opposite of many men his age. He was an exclamation point where his counterparts were question marks.

And I supposed he *had* to be stretched up so taut, because the very thing he carried depended on his stability.

A big, hunkin', gallon-sized water bottle.

On top of his head.

Almost completely full.

Its label had been shorn off, and it was the kind of receptacle one buys in bulk when stocking up for parties or earthquake kits. The bottle had morphed from transparent to translucent, probably having weathered this very trail a handful of times before.

An easy smile adorned his face as he strode ahead, making conversation with his wife. He had an effervescence to him, a kid-like joy where he knew other eyes were glued to his headpiece, yet he gave not a single damn.

In fact, he reveled in the delicate balance that was keeping a giant water bottle atop one's noggin, not just to practice his own balance, but to practice the art of having fun. The art of play.

Seeing him surfaced a memory of how I saw the world through seven-year-old eyes. My parents and I had just moved to America and spent many summer days walking around Washington, DC, taking in the tall monuments, the friendly, smiling faces, and the newness of an uprooted life.

Because I was a young kid, my existence was predominantly painted in the *carefree* and *mirth* colors. It was easy to *be* because I had far fewer important things to *do*.

Skipping down the National Mall?

Why not?

Cartwheeling on the lawn of the Natural History Museum?

Why not?

Pretending I was a tightrope walker inching my way across the vastness of the Grand Canyon?

"Мама, пожалуйста купи мне бутылку воды!"

Not yet knowing a lick of English, I implored my mom to buy me a bottle of water to complete my ultra-balancing act. She has always been the type of mother to support my dreams, whether imagined or real, and approved the purchase, admittedly for her child to avoid heatstroke. Equipment acquired, I began my delicate journey across the soiled sidewalk—or the rope stretched across canyon edges.

I gingerly placed the water bottle atop my head to initiate the act. Since the plastic bottle was small and flimsy, I had to keep readjusting it in my nest of hair as it slid down. My arms were splayed out to form a T, and my legs danced knowingly, one in front of the other. Carefully, I began to walk.

It was a heroic act to tread even a few feet with the bottle balanced on my head, and I imagined smashing world records for longest tightrope walk.

Katya Davydova, the ultra-balancer, wins again! Watch that posture: stick straight! And ladies and gentlemen, there's a water bottle atop her head! She's done it. Bravo, bravo!

In my mind, an invisible audience cheered. In the streets, a few passersby smiled at my own ebullient mother, clapping at her daughter's carefree mirth.

I'd made it to the other side of the canyon and jumped joyously, holding my water bottle up to the sky as my medal.

So, when did the bottle tumble? When did I fall?

When did my inner child start hiding from wonder and instead fall in line with the *shoulds* of the world?

We shouldn't live in the clouds. We have responsibilities. You can be carefree only when you've done your chores. Work comes before play. You should walk normally. These were the messages I'd been hearing—and telling myself—for the last few decades.

What happened?

What happened is I started running at Runyon to offset my big lunch instead of just exploring a new environment. I am an adult after all, and adults need regular doses of exercise.

Bonus points for variety in types of workouts and levels of difficulty. This run checked all the boxes.

What happened is I ate the same lunch as yesterday and the day before that and the day before *that* because it's more efficient to meal prep once a week than cook every day. God forbid I explore new recipes simply to try new flavors or because it's fun to create questionably edible creations in the kitchen on a whim.

What happened is I suggested to my partner we build a fort in our living room—*hey, let's remember what it's like to be a kid!*—and we never did. It was too impractical to move all the furniture and clean the floors and set everything back to their tidy, assigned places.

I'd noticed myself doing some things because they had a "because." As a logical, reasoning adult, I'd told myself to exercise because it's good for me, to meal prep because it saves time, to build a fort later because it's inconvenient now.

As kid Katya, I'd balanced on my imaginary tightrope *just because.*

The image of my seven-year-old self melted away as I refocused attention on the passing gentleman with that absurd water jug on his head. Here was a man walking on his own tightrope stretched across a canyon—be it Grand or Runyon.

He knew.

He knew the truth adults are just big kids, with big responsibilities. But he also knew with great responsibility comes the even greater need for *play*. So play he did.

Cracking the biggest smile through less-than-white teeth and dry lips, I mentally thanked him for reminding me *shoulds* find their homes in the depths of those canyons, imagined or real.

The things we carry atop our heads are a clue to how we carry *ourselves*, whether mired in moroseness or mirth, free to care or carefree.

That purposeful, public ridiculousness—balancing a water bottle when it's not a very "adult" thing to do—is precisely the key to our own childhoods. It's play. It's being human.

And we forget.

We forget our livelihoods and instead buy designer clothes and designer water bottles, thinking our riches will make us rich.

Inevitably, they don't.

This man knew this and carried *himself* in a way that allowed him to step through that door back to childhood, back to when it made sense to be a tightrope walker. Back to when we wouldn't give a damn about the passing glances, about the implicit *shoulds* and *should-nots*.

I wish I could tell you I went back to Runyon the following week (I did) and carried my own water bottle atop my head, not giving a single damn. (I did not.)

My first excuse was I don't carry water when I run (fair), but what about the cooldown? That second evening at Runyon, I intentionally spent an extra half hour walking around the neighborhood with a forty-eight-ounce monstrosity of an off-brand Hydroflask. The thing I carried wasn't designer, and it wasn't decrepit either, but it also only found its home in my hand. My head sat empty.

I found an inviting grassy hill overlooking a community garden and the sparkling city below and plopped down. Beautiful people passed by, clutching leashes or bottles. They were either preoccupied with their phones or mentally somewhere else. I'd imagined them sorting their to-do lists for the week ahead, ruminating on a recent date, or spinning in the cycle of the *shoulds* they'd built up for themselves.

As I sat there, the memory of the jolly white-haired man from the previous week popped into my brain. If I couldn't carry a thing atop my head and *play*, perhaps I could carry *myself* in a way that allowed me to feel that effervescence of childhood once more.

So, I leaned back and at once felt cradled by the soft grass of the gentle slope at my back. I inhaled the earthy musk and smiled to myself.

We shouldn't live in the clouds. We have responsibilities. You can be carefree only when you've done your chores. Work comes before play. You should lay down normally.

As if drawn by magnets, my hands and feet flew upward, and I began to dance like an overturned bug. Eyes closed, I leisurely glided my knees and elbows, making swirls against the sherbet sky.

I figured park onlookers glanced in my direction, but I hoped they smiled instead of glared. I hoped the way I carried myself at that moment, supported by firm soil and buoyed by the levity of kid-like fascination, was play.

I opened my eyes and imagined shapes in the clouds, high above the tightrope walkers back down on Earth.

CAT LESSONS

―

From my usual spot on the couch, I observe as Pascal strides into the living room with gusto, happy from his nap, stretches out all four limbs and back, and plops down on the hardwood floor.

He is beauty, he is grace, and he is my teacher.

He's not exactly how I envisioned a source of wisdom to look like, though.

His limbs end in sharp, milky claws, and his whiskers, cashmere-pink nose, and emerald eyes give him quite the dignified countenance.

He communicates with me in nasally "mcgow!" rivaling the best operatic tenor. Every day without fail, he leaps onto the bathroom counter and headbutts everything in sight, then purrs happily, all snuggled up in the sink.

Ever since moving in with my partner, I've had the privilege to learn from this six-year-old cat and his two brothers,

Charlie and Mars. Having grown up with two cats, I thought I knew what to expect: they sleep a lot, they eat a lot, and they appreciate affection, if only on their terms.

There's a joke in the pet community: people own dogs, but cats own people. These mighty felines dictate when to be stroked, when to be left alone, and where—precisely—they want scratches. Otherwise, one may find cups knocked over, needy noses as magnets to whatever food is on a fork, and, if unlucky, red ribbons on human arms and legs.

These cats are different.

Not only are Pascal, Charlie, and Mars the sweetest, most loving kitties I've ever owned, but also prime examples of how to live.

What could humans learn from felines that their big brains and smartphones didn't already know?

You see, I had just started a new, demanding job where I had to be "on" and presenting leadership development skills to managers for about eight hours a day. Simultaneously, my partner Nick and I were figuring out our personal dynamics in how to meld our wildly divergent living styles.

While our love for the kitties was unwavering from either side, we had differences of opinion on things like the merit of mornings, kitchen cleanliness, and the best way to eat a sandwich. I was also acclimating to a new neighborhood, fulfilling my commitment to daily workouts and healthy habits, and, of course, writing this book.

With three decades of perfectionism coursing through my veins, I was used to making every minute productive, and optimizing my time to pursue whatever goals I was chasing. It was difficult to find a moment of zen to just *be*, not *do*.

About a year ago, when we were still living separately, Nick listened to my rolodex of stresses seemingly every week.

One particular day, I'd called him crying in the middle of my driveway workout because I was feeling too weak to do one hundred kettlebell swings, even though I'd "only" worked an arduous ten-hour day.

Why couldn't I get the gumption to finish this workout?

"Okay, Katya, here's what I want you to do," he said through my whimpers.

Great! I thought. *I like doing things!*

"Just take five minutes to sit and do nothing."

Do nothing? I balked.

"Nick, what does that even mean? How does one simply *do nothing*? There are a million things to be done, and 'nothing' isn't one of them!"

So, I continued to run on my hamster wheel and burn myself out.

Later, I came to realize what Nick had meant—and had been practicing as a way to slow down *his* own whirlwind work life—was to carve out increments without screens, without stimulation, without expectation.

What I *didn't* realize was he had three little helpers. Three furry creatures who encouraged him to unplug and be present.

"Aw, Mars, are you so exhausted from your nap?" We like to tease the kitties, and Mars especially consistently retorts back.

I knew napping was a feline's favorite activity, but when I started working from home and spending a good chunk of my time with the cats, I saw firsthand how crucial sleep was for them.

They *needed* rest, and lots of it, but they weren't napping out of laziness necessarily. I observed periods of supreme concentration in catching the latest bug, high-speed, post-poop zoomies back and forth across the apartment, and acrobatic flips during a shoelace chase unparalleled by the best gymnast.

Then: sleep.

High-intensity activity, high-quality rest. Rinse and repeat.

In my own human model, there was high-intensity activity, followed by low-intensity activity, followed by—you guessed it—more high-intensity activity. Rest only came in seven-to-eight-hour periods where I would wake up tired only to rev up the wheels again. That low-intensity activity was of terrible quality too: scrolling through Instagram, milling about trying to decide what project to tackle next, and feeling exhausted by the end.

It was a recipe for burnout.

When the five of us moved in together, I began to discover how to make space for deliberate rest. During work, after finishing facilitating my first two-hour long workshop of the day, I would find a cat (and even better if all three were in the same room), and intentionally talk to them, give them rubs and armpit massages (Mars' favorite!), and take a refreshing swim in their green eyes.

Somehow, the chatter of my monkey mind would dim and we'd exchange oxytocin from our snuggles. Refreshed, I'd go to my next task.

What's ironic is at my organization, which focuses on research-based behavioral change in the workplace, I was teaching managers and executives the importance of making time to deliberately recharge.

In fact, several times a week, I would emphatically make the argument to slow down "because our brain works best in spurts of high-intensity activity, followed by high-quality rest."

The managers would all nod in agreement on the Zoom screen.

Where else had I seen that model before?

Grabbing Mars and holding his little furry body in a gentle hug, I began practicing what I preached. With every cuddle, I invited more high-quality rest to just *be*.

"Aw, Pascal, biiiiig stretch!"

Over the past few months, I've found myself remarking on the cats' stretching habits at least once a day. I noticed every single time they would wake up from a nap, they would methodically stretch out their front paws in child's pose, then arch their backs in the eponymous cat stretch, and finally finish off by elongating their hind paws. If they were laying on the floor, just enjoying the silence of *being*, they'd form an upside-down rainbow with their furry bodies, ensuring their backs stayed limber.

It became evident cats are naturally inclined to be in tune with their somatic self. They *feel* how their bodies feel, and calibrate to find optimal comfort by stretching.

We as humans, too, take care of our bodies: we eat well, we exercise, we go on mindful walks. Paragons of health.

Ha! Who am I kidding?

The majority of us can't even remember the last time we asked our body how it feels. I know I sure don't.

Typically, I'm tied to my laptop, either sitting in a less-than-er-gonomic chair or sprawled on the couch when I'm not facilitating workshops. I don't even notice my shoulders creeping up and closing the gap between themselves and my ears.

Too often I catch myself holding my breath, focused so intently on a project I literally forget to exhale. Even my eyesight becomes blurry, because my contact lenses get so dry from the lack of blinking. The stiff concentration leaves no room for body contemplation.

Our cats, on the other hand, use every opportunity they have to tune in to the acute awareness of their physical selves to elongate their limbs and provide immediate bodily relief.

How does it come so instinctively for them?

That might be the wrong question to ask.

Research posits *most* mammals stretch instinctively, particularly in "transitions between biological behaviors, especially the sleep-wake rhythm" (Bertolucci 2011). This is called pandiculation.

All that is a fancy way of saying animals, including humans, subconsciously stretch and yawn after waking up to stimulate their soft tissue and muscles. We do it not only because it feels good, but also because it helps our bodies get ready to respond to the stimuli in the world.

If this stretching behavior is hard-wired into cats *and* humans, why do I regularly find myself neglecting the urge?

It's because I don't make myself aware of it. The brain over-rides the body, and I am left stiff.

So, I've made a new rule for myself. Any time I see Charlie, Mars, or Pascal do a big stretch, I do it right there with them. And I whisper to myself, "Aw, Katya, biiiiiig stretch!"

"Aw, Charlie, you're so snuggled up!"

It's seven in the morning, just thirty minutes before my alarm is due to ring, and I ease myself out of a delicious slumber by stretching out my limbs like a starfish.

Clearly, I've internalized the lesson from Pascal. My partner Nick is still sleeping, mouth set in a hint of a smile, because there's a warm little being between us.

Charlie, the most playful and adventurous of the brothers, has a beautiful ability to find home in the earthquakes in the canyon of our bodies. Almost every morning, he'll lodge himself tightly between Nick and me, and as we shift around, he'll weather the storm, shifting, too, but always coming back to look up at us, doe-eyed in contentment.

I gaze into his half-closed eyes, his front paws clutching his back paws in an impossibly tight ball, and stroke the space between his ears gently. Like clockwork, he'll hop up on our bed around 5 a.m., and stay there for the next few hours, changing positions as often as we do.

Every morning, he *knows* this space and time between us is not without hiccups, not without landscape changes or the possibility of getting squished between his humans, but he does it anyway. He seeks out moments of comfort and safety in uncanny places and fully surrenders.

Whether via nature or nurture, Charlie has learned to be the master of hygge. It's a Danish and Norwegian word that exemplifies true, intentional coziness and bliss. Think of wearing your softest pair of pajamas, sitting by a crackling fire, swaddled in toasty blankets, with a cup of hot chocolate warming both your hands, while snow gently pads the roof of your remote cabin. All is well, and you are present.

I crave this idealistic scene, unburdened by life's demands.

Watching Charlie reposition himself for the umpteenth time that morning, however, I realize two things: Life will always have demands, and I don't have to travel to snowy Norway to find comfort.

Those demands can wait.

In the morning, I can find comfort in the slowness of sipping my almond milk coffee on a blissful Sunday, with the distracting smartphone out of sight and out of mind in the other room, and instead my attention on the waking world past my window.

At night, I can find comfort in lighting a lemon-and-sage candle from Aldi and delighting in the fact its periwinkle wax produces a warm glow that makes shadows dance on walls.

Between teaching workshops, I can find comfort in tending to my indoor radishes, peppers, and zinnias, gently patting down the soil of newly sown seeds and misting them with life-giving water.

Finally, I can slow down time and find comfort in laying my head next to Pascal's sprawling belly, with Charlie at my feet and Mars snuggled into the bend in my waist, and surrender to the warm rumble of *purr*-fection.

This is what the cats have shown me so far. To rest, to stretch, and to find pockets of bliss.

By *being*, Mars, Pascal, and Charlie are teaching me a thing or two about *living*.

UNDERWEAR

———

Every woman I know has period underwear. Ragged, ratty triangular clumps of fabric barely held together by their constituent threads. We wear them every month when we feel less than glorious, when emotions rise and moods fall. We wear them when we want our garments to match the broiling of the seas they're covering.

Each lunar cycle, we allow them to get stained, soaked in garnet, only to relinquish their hold on our blood at the end of the week.

Rinse and repeat.

The thing about my period underwear is they've been in rotation for years. And I mean *years*, in a manner that's embarrassing enough to be put in italics. You see, I tend to hold onto things the exact opposite way I shed my endometrium every month.

Particularly sentimental are relics of dates with past boyfriends: an old bar napkin where we had nerded out on calculus equations, a tattered wristband from that one show in Richmond, a seashell from our second date at the beach.

And while my underwear are definitely not on my list of objects I keep close to my heart, they are the things that grace my skin most closely and most intimately.

Because these cotton masses have seen the passing of so much time, they are in various states of disrepair. Some have elastic divorced from their fabric. Some have holes in places where the sun don't shine, and never will, because I cannot show them to anyone. They're to be kept under wraps, under the dark security of a pair of jeans or a long dress.

People say to keep your friends close and your enemies closer. I say keep your period underwear as close to you as possible, where no one can access them. So far, that's worked out well for me.

One spring morning, my boyfriend Nick and I were getting ready to enjoy a beautiful California day sauntering through the arts district. At that point, we'd been dating for almost two years and would frequently sleep over at each other's apartments. We'd come to know and trust each other at a comfortable level.

However, every time it was *that time of the month*, I'd turn away from him to change. No one saw my period under-wear, *ever*.

As we were getting ready on this particular morning, I stole a moment to slip on my jeans without Nick noticing.

Still under the covers, he called out, "Hey love, can you throw me a pair?"

Because I was standing by Nick's dresser, I reached into the top drawer and plunged into the dark hues. It struck me as curious men's underwear is generally unremarkable and monochromatic. *We have a mission to protect the crown jewels! We must adorn the butts and balls of men in hues that match the severity of the business!*

Then: a spark of color. Beneath a deep sea of grays and navies, a hint of turquoise and cream caught my attention. *Hmm. I've never seen these before.* My eyes held onto the striped pattern as my fingers fished for the soft material.

Out came ragged, ratty, rectangular fabric barely held together by its constituent threads, the kind that is not seen by others' eyes.

His period underwear.

"Here you go!" I exclaimed with more glee than even *I* expected, chucking the colorful ball of cotton at Nick's chest.

As soon as it left my hand, the world jolted into stillness. My eyes dilated.

Oh, shit.

Should I have dug that deep? What if he wanted me to grab one of the dozens of dark pairs on top? Maybe he intentionally hid this particular pair for no eyes to see?!

For a split second, I imagined a role reversal: Nick standing by *my* dresser, plunging his hands deep into *my* underwear drawer. I balked at the thought of asking him to toss me a pair. *No one saw my period underwear, ever.* I wondered if he'd felt this was a violation of trust.

His voice broke my anxious spiral.

"Oh yeah! I forgot I had those!" he said with amusement and a smile.

As I watched him shimmy on the worn-out underwear, I reflected on the slew of vulnerabilities we'd already shared with one another. That time he let his shirt and neck absorb my snot and tears as the weight of the world crashed down. That time I enveloped him curled up on the couch, absorbing his heaving sobs after his grandfather died.

We got to see the parts we hid from others. *That was vulnerability. That was trust.*

Since then, we'd moved in together. We are privy to the strange and marvelous idiosyncrasies of living with another human being.

Best of all, we do laundry together. We mix piles of our period underwear and see all the stains, the holes, the fabric divorced from itself.

It is one of the threads tying us together.

THE CONSTELLATIONS ON OUR SKIN

———

To know someone is to trace the constellations on their skin.

As a kid, I wondered why my best friend Oksana had so many freckles on her shoulders and arms. It was as if burnt-orange dust had been sprinkled on top of her body and made its eternal home there. *Why didn't I have such a pattern?*

Oksana and I grew up together because our moms had been best friends since *they* were nine years old, and the tradition carried on into the next generation. Being a few years older, she's seen me develop from an infant to filling out my own un-freckled skin.

Every time we'd go on family vacations to the beach—Orlando, Myrtle, Ocean City—she'd leave with more freckles than she started with that day.

By the tenth straight hour of swimming and lounging in infinite sunshine, our conversations would only deepen. It was as if the sun would draw out more of her essence; she'd share her inner patterns of thoughts and develop her outer patterns of freckles.

"Oh look, you have one there!" I'd point to the tiny new specks on her face.

The next day they would be covered with makeup.

Although we had no shared biology, we spent a lot of time together because we were only children with intertwined family histories. In fact, Oksana's parents won the same green card lottery as mine, thanks to the Diversity Immigrant Visa program.

Out of the millions of applicants in 1999, my family was part of the 0.01 percent who were granted rights to immigrate to the US (Results of the Diversity Immigrant Visa Program 1998; Statistical Yearbook of the Immigration and Naturalization Service 2002, 24). A few years later, imagine our shock when we found out—through a costly cross-continental phone call— our closest family friends were headed stateside.

More astoundingly, they settled in Virginia, in a neighboring city just fifteen minutes away.

As my big sister by choice, Oksana introduced me to many milestones of being a teenager in the early 2000s. We holed up in her bedroom or mine, depending on the week, and blasted Good Charlotte or Avril Lavigne to sing discordantly into hairbrushes. We memorized every line of the first Harry Potter movie and spoke with British accents to each other, casting imaginary spells that invoked the magic of figuring out who we were.

She'd wear butterfly earrings in her double-pierced ears, sew her own clothing, and style her hair in a thousand different ways to match the musician of the month in her growing CD collection. I'd don my "punk" bracelets and studded belts, give myself kohl raccoon eyes, and distill adolescence through Green Day lyrics.

While we were so eager to peacock to the world we were indeed cool, we kept quite a bit hidden from the public.

Namely, our faces.

Both Oksana and I were plagued with acne throughout our childhood and early adulthood, and tried every which way to not let the world know.

"Okay, here's what you do. See this concealer stick? That goes under your eyes and on your pimples," she would instruct.

"Then," she'd say, reaching into her bottomless makeup bag for the iconic air-puffed foundation that was a staple for many American teenage girls in the 2000s, "you spread this on your face."

In the safety of her bathroom, I made note of her green-tinted creams to combat redness, her blush to artificially breathe life into her cheeks, and the vast array of lip glosses to shine attention on soft parts of our faces that did not house craters.

For Oksana, attending school meant spending precious minutes each morning covering up all those blemishes, blackheads, and freckles with swaths of fair-colored makeup. For me, it was much of the same: dot those zits with concealer, apply a shield of beige across the face, and ring some eyeliner and lip shine around their corresponding features.

We didn't want others to see all the inflamed turmoil underneath.

The fondest moments, though, were when we revealed ourselves to each other through lenses of our past, present, and future.

We reminisced about our childhood in our home country: guffawing about the day I farted right on her face, as revenge for stealing my doll. She shares a different version of the story to this day. However, we both remembered what it was like to stand in line for a loaf of bread, holding our mothers' hand—and how refreshing it was to have food security in the States.

I'd ask her for advice on how to navigate the domain of having a boyfriend, and she'd confide in me her own relationship secrets. At family gatherings, we'd squirrel away to a bedroom to both bemoan and giggle about teenage romance, and when an adult would inevitably come up to call us down for dessert, we'd answer their raised eyebrows and "What are you talking about?" with a chorus of "Nothing!"

We also planned for our futures: What would happen after high school? After college? Grad school? When she left for university while I was still in high school, I took solace in the fact my big sister would share all her wisdom in trailblazing this new path forward.

In those tiny, seemingly inconsequential moments while laughing hysterically over our seventh rewatch of *Prisoner of Azkaban*, I'd glance to my left and be strangely comforted by the little red bumps on my sister's face. For two people who were so close by circumstance and choice instead of by blood, I loved we shared that vulnerability to be barefaced.

Maybe our faces were mirrors. Physically, our eyes saw the same inflamed spots on one another. But through our intertwined connection and history shared by no one else in our respective friend groups, we saw through to the sisterhood—the full spectrum of milestones and heartbreaks—underneath.

As we blossomed into adults, our acne subsided and we began wearing less and less coverup. Oksana still periodically mentioned she hated her freckles and would hide them occasionally. I, on the other hand, especially after moving to sunny Los Angeles, watched with glee as my own nose became peppered with them.

How could she still be so averse to the tiny skin constellations that augmented her beauty?

I wondered if she knew about the latest trend of tattooing freckles on noses and cheeks. Seeing young girls with fake freckles in the streets of LA and on social media made me ponder, *Would Oksana one day embrace her skin?*

Because of our now long-distance friendship—her in Maryland and me in California—we had to figure out how to maintain our kindred closeness.

Every Tuesday, we call each other for an hour, covering the full spectrum of mundane to extraordinary, and share secrets only sisters can know: our past, our present, our future.

We were learning to show up in the world as our true, unconcealed selves. We cheered each other on in setting boundaries and leaving unsavory workplaces, on navigating frustration and love with our respective boyfriends, on being brave enough to surface our fear and excitement about the future. I coached her through saying "no" at work; she coached me through saying "yes" to regular date nights.

We continued to show up raw to one another. We took pride in growing into our skin.

The other day during our weekly phone call, Oksana said, "I haven't worn makeup in over three months! It feels so free."

I nodded emphatically and yelled, "Yes! I love hearing you say that!"

What a quiet joy it was to know my sister stopped hiding herself. She finally let the world in on her own constellations.

Unlike Oksana, my boyfriends never gave a second thought to covering their pimples or freckles.

"Oh look, you have one there!" I'd point to a freckle on the rib of one guy I briefly dated.

Tracing my fingers on his smooth skin, I found myself on a mini galactic adventure, an astronaut exploring the space of his now prostrate body.

He didn't say a word.

"You've got Orion on your back," I tried again.

Again, pregnant silence.

We exchanged physical warmth for those few weeks but not much else. I tried to outline the story of his constellations, to understand what his outer patterns would reveal about his internal patterns of thought. The stars were too dim.

His inner beauty was a glint in the sky, shiny, tempting, but too far to reach.

So we let go.

The stars on his skin faded from memory like smog blanketing the city's twinkling skyscrapers.

Months later, I countered my shivers by inching closer to the warm body to my left. We were laying on top of blankets that took the sting out of gravel on a roadside pull-off, deep in the Angeles National Forest.

The chill was surprisingly bitter for October, so we smushed our sides tightly together. The air was still, a stark contrast to the honks and sirens of a typical city night. All I could hear were the periodic whooshes of the wind and the deep breaths of the man next to me.

When I met Nick, I immediately noticed the two freckles on his otherwise symmetrical face, both on his left cheek. He was on the quieter side, so I gushed to him about my love for astronomy on our first date, trying to reveal the shiny bits of myself. On that initial encounter, I had worn gold shadow on my eyelids reminiscent of glimmering stars. On our fifth date to the forest, I went barefaced.

Laying on the blanket, our eyes were glued to the heavens. I had invited him to watch a meteor shower and explained where in the sky to catch the shooting stars.

"Meteor showers are named after the constellation they emanate from," I started. "See those three little dots in a diagonal row?"

A deep murmur of acknowledgment.

"That's the belt. They'll come from Orion himself."

And so they did. During our few hours looking skyward, we made a game of "who saw that shooting star first." I was the avid sky gazer, pointing out the milky splashes of Cassiopeia and Pleiades, but he was beating me in his meteor count.

"Did you make a wish?" I whispered.

A long tail streaked by, igniting blackness.

I heard the crinkle of his smile through the upturned corners of his mouth as he leaned his head further up against mine.

Years later, I steal moments in the morning when Nick hasn't yet stirred awake. I gaze at the space of his back, expanding outward with each breath, a tiny supernova combusting every few seconds.

There, I see clusters of freckles for which I have no name yet. There is the map of my human: colors inverted from the night sky, dark specks in patterns splashed against a backdrop of light. Maybe I won't find Orion, but in time, constellations will emerge.

Nick sighs and turns to face me, still serene in the diaphanous lull of sleep.

I note the two freckles on his left cheek and look down at my own bare arms.

Huh.

Oh, look. I have one there.

And there. And there. And there.

My bronzed skin holds patterns of freckles I'd failed to notice recently, and far more of them. *Must be the California sun.*

I wonder if my freckles have a mirrored twin on his skin, a shared mark on a knee or hip. A testament to the history we've built.

To the nights when I've collapsed into him, sobbing in staccato at the overwhelm of being a person. To the nights he's done the same. To feeding me and helping me to the bathroom after a surgery to excise a tumor, only four months into dating. To sharing narratives of our respective stories and feeling how vulnerably beautiful it was to weave our own history together.

We see each other's skin-deep constellations and dive into the universe that is below. Most days, I wear no makeup around him.

It's a quarter past eight, and I trace my thumb lightly on the two stars on his cheek.

His eyes flutter open, then shut in pretend anguish at seeing the sun so bright. I drape my tanned arm over his side and pull myself closer, looking up.

Nestled, he leisurely opens both eyes and looks directly into mine.

"You're the most beautiful girl in the world," he whispers as I think about the crust on my lashes and the zit on my cheek.

My eyes radiate love as I notice, for the millionth time, yellow freckles against the backdrop of green.

Sunflower eyes, I call them.

I close mine briefly and think how lucky I am to have a lover right here, and a sister three thousand miles away. These are my people. I know their perfectly imperfect patterns on heavenly skin. They know mine.

A warmth spreads between Nick and me, sparks flying like Orion's meteors from all those years ago. Our fingers waltz across the star clusters on our faces and backs, gaze still held steady. Our faces are bare and familiar, a comfort, a home to welcome and cherish every sunrise and sunset.

We sink back into the depth of slumber for just five more minutes. We've got miles to go to trace the constellations on our skin.

YOUR SILENCE
IS FULLNESS

———

Your silence is fullness.

Oddly enough, you wouldn't stop talking on our first date. Snuggled into the cozy, orange, velvet couch at a low-lit, seventies-inspired bar, I inched myself microscopically closer to you as you unraveled your life's threads.

I'd asked you about the guitar from your dating app profile picture. You'd looked serious, composed, focused on whatever chord progression you were dreaming up next.

"Let me see your calluses." My eyes lit up slyly as I tried to keep my voice steady.

I knew what I was doing, yet butterflies danced in my stomach.

You slid over your hand—a gift—and finished tracing a brief synopsis of your musical years while I traced the hardened skin of your palm.

Here is why you picked up the guitar. Here is why you haven't put it down in decades. And right here, on your right-hand fingers, was evidence of skin and string kissing violently as you pressed individual notes on the fretboard into a song.

I found it fascinating you were left-handed, having had to adapt your playing and living to a right-hander's world.

Luckily, our respective dominant palms met, and we clasped onto one another, smiling like we'd just shared a secret. There was an easy ember growing warmer between us.

By the time midnight struck, our bodies were coursing with liquid courage. As you were signing the check, I dared you to steal an orange from the bar.

"You wouldn't," I teased.

A flash of your deft left hand, and you proved me wrong.

While neither of us had kleptomaniac tendencies, you just couldn't pass up my challenge. I couldn't help but linger on your mischievous grin.

We walked back to my house through the empty streets of Hollywood at two in the morning on a Tuesday—now Wednesday—and devoured the juicy fruit. I licked the citrus

nectar running down my hand and licked your face. That's
how your nickname was born: Salty.

A curious medley of opposites: education, careers, families,
ways of being. *What else would I learn from you?*

On our second date that following weekend, we spent sixteen
hours together, double that of our first date. It was then, lying
on a blanket overlooking the Pacific Ocean, I drowned in the
green silence of your eyes.

We'd both just shared painful details of our lives growing up,
raw stories usually kept hidden until months down the line,
until safety and trust of handling such delicate glimpses into
our humanness had been established.

But this was different.

It was in the silence that followed we reified space for one another.
Lying on our stomachs facing each other, our side profiles inches
apart, our silence said more than words could convey.

I hear you. I see you. I know what it's like.

I felt my ears and cheeks blossom with crimson, and hoped
you'd think it was the sun's pernicious doing. *From all the
words I could choose from three languages right now, their lack
felt most right.* Our silence was full-bodied, warm.

We nuzzled into each other and inhaled the salty ocean air.
Our embers swelled.

Sometimes, your silence would be maddeningly deafening. Riding in your car along the coastline to some weekend adventure, I'd sit and sit and sit, waiting for you to ask a question or carry a conversation. By that point, I'd tried topics old and new. I'd gleefully tried pointing out roadside attractions as colored blurs. Our soundtrack remained the hum of tires on asphalt.

Among my friends, I'm known as the listener, skilled at asking precise questions and being a sounding board for their sorrows and joys. My career in organizational psychology and leadership facilitation has also made me extremely comfortable with silence. Sometimes, I'll ask a particularly drop-the-mic question of the workshop group, and we'll sit and sit and sit until someone punctures the stillness with their voice.

"Take your time," I say. "We're here to squirm through this thinking time together."

But I was the one squirming in the passenger seat as the minutes passed, your eyes on the road and your mind in a universe of its own. Words, especially of affirmation, were my love language, and it felt unsettling to not receive them or have them land with you.

"Love," I'd start. "What's on your mind?"

You would sigh, and out would tumble a flurry of worries about work. Stress stifled you as you sifted through the rolodex of *what ifs* and *how can wes*.

"It's not you; it's never you," you assured me. "I know I haven't been engaging much lately, and I'm sorry. This week wore me down."

I'd squeeze your hand, palm to palm, giving you space and time to process.

While you were an internal processor, I needed to speak my worries through. I'd share big and little things with the urgency of soap bubbles about to pop, from some discomfort at work, to meatier existential questions.

Sometimes you'd engage with a rapid-fire volley of thoughts, sometimes you'd simply say "mmm" as if to chew on it. Sometimes I'd wonder if you thought I talked too much.

Interestingly, as soon as you started on a topic that enthralled you—music, computers, worldly matters—you would orate like a professor, seemingly endlessly. If I didn't understand something, you'd provide context, analogies, and attempt different angles to make the convoluted clear.

The first time you met my mother, only about a month after we started dating, we three sat down to a home-cooked meal in my tiny apartment. Upon her questioning, you dove into an hour of explaining bitcoin, complete with diagrams on printer paper scattered among empty plates.

A few days later, I casually mentioned how my mom and I both appreciated your gentle, thorough approach to engaging us in conversation about technology so foreign to us.

"You know, Katya, I usually don't talk that much," you replied.

That took me by wild surprise.

"What do you mean?"

Here was a person who, despite being so inwardly tuned, derived energy by sharing his knowledge and wisdom for hours on end.

You explained you spent most of your childhood alone, exploring the woods and creek behind your house. You'd lose yourself in the trees and find your way home along the train tracks, just like you would lose yourself in the infinite worlds of books. Your older brothers didn't really listen to you, and your parents were too busy, so you escaped to places where spoken words were of little consequence.

So, what a gift it was, I thought, to revel in silence together.

As we continued evolving as individuals and as a pair, the nature of our silences shifted.

Six months after we started dating, the pandemic and its associated lockdowns and loneliness hit. Around the same time, the company I worked for endured a massive merger, and while I was fortunate enough to survive two rounds of layoffs, I was now doing the job of several people. If, before, a team led learning and development for a company of 250, now I was at the helm for four hundred people, in addition to my prior job responsibilities.

Being constantly *on* while not being able to de-stress with friends took a toll on my health. The bags under my eyes got darker. My hair thinned. My calendar, usually brimming with bar nights and hikes, was now a sea of endless meetings to create initiatives to support our burnt-out employees.

You, too, experienced your share of work challenges. Sometimes you'd call me about it. Other times, you'd keep silent, bubbled up until you burst under pressure.

And then, they found a tumor. My first concern was whether I'd be able to get back to work quickly enough. My second was whether you could take a day off to accompany me to the hospital.

When I woke up in the recovery ward, the first thing I said to you was concerning the miracle of modern medicine.

"Science is so cool! *So cool!* Can you believe it?" I croaked, still groggy, as they wheeled me into the recovery room.

You'd been at the hospital with me since seven in the morning, and it was now afternoon. We didn't end up leaving until ten at night, since I kept slipping in and out of consciousness, in and out of pain loops.

There you were, sitting right by me, holding my hand or stroking my head. I didn't say much; for once, my voice-box had no energy to produce.

You didn't either, except for the occasional "You're doin' so good, love" to enliven my spirits.

Your silence was fullness, a cocoon softer and more enveloping than the haze of drugs and the worn-out hospital blanket tucked around me.

Those moments of heavy silence were some of the most powerful magnets pulling us closer and opening further channels of trust.

I felt held.

As the pandemic wore on, my core circle tightened. I was seeing you and my roommate consistently, but it was harder to engage with strangers, having to resort to masked head nods to passersby or just a brief "hi, there" to folks in the grocery store.

I'd been so used to making serendipitous connections almost everywhere I went. Now, I missed the sounds of lively chatter.

So, I resolved myself to getting lost in podcasts, audiobooks, music, something to fill the air with a human voice. Even though the world stilled, silence—nourishing, meaningful silence—was hard to come by.

To be fair, I avoided silence, avoided sitting still. Despite my extroverted tendencies, I craved alone time, but as soon as I was by myself, I resorted to either working, working on side projects, or doom scrolling as a means to cope.

I became a human *doing*.

What was it like to be a human *being* again?

You tried to tell me how: "Katya, I just want you to sit for five minutes. I want you to do absolutely nothing. Don't look at your phone, don't listen to music, don't call a friend, don't even think about turning on your latest audiobook at double speed. Just be still."

What?

Intellectually, I knew what you were saying. I knew the benefits of *being*.

But it was so antithetical to my upbringing of constantly achieving, accomplishing, being on the go to the next and the next and the next. I did not know how to pause and sit in the silence of the absence of it all.

That is, until you sat with me.

We moved in together and planted roots on your gray couch. Sometimes, during the workday after finishing our lunch, we'd just sit and digest in quiet company.

I'd feel those old urges to ask you what was on your mind—a penny for your thoughts—much like I did during those early road trip dates.

And sometimes, you'd spill the latest round of stresses at work with dulled emotions to steel yourself against them.

Other times, you'd look over at me, taking the last bite of my vegetable stir-fry, smile softly, and say, "I'm not really thinking about anything."

What a joy that seemed like, to empty your mind of *to-dos, have-tos,* and *shoulds.*

What else would I learn from you?

The months of living together have been comprised of delicious laughter, a few even-keeled disagreements, and a medley of strange noises we didn't expect to hear from a fellow human.

We meow to our cats, we meow to each other, we create a whole new vocabulary from inside jokes and write them down on the refrigerator whiteboard.

I sigh in contentment when you come up behind me for a surprise hug, and you purr in appreciation when I massage the kinks in your back as you wash dishes.

We sing songs together, holler at the tops of our lungs (but not so much our neighbors get mad), we voice ourselves to each other. We use words and speak up.

But interspersed between those moments of expression are the even more precious moments of quiet.

We pass winks to each other down the long hallway connecting opposite ends of our house. We cook together to the tune of the chop-chop of zucchini and the sizzle of chicken in the pan: a jazz assortment of life domestic. We sit on that worn gray couch and observe our kittens snuggling in boxes or chairs or right between our own bodies. We watch the plants grow, luxuriating in the time of *being*, minutes oozing slowly. We hold space for each other, stroking heads, hands, and bodies, a wordless, ginger sign of care.

Palm to palm, forehead to forehead, our mutual quiet speaks volumes. A glowing ember of love smolders between us, unspoken yet felt so deeply. Our silence is fullness, one that fills me up like no voices ever could.

EXTREME HAWAIIAN ALOHA

Here's the funny thing about cat litter:

Its intended users don't give a shit.

Have you ever wondered what goes on in the corporate offices of Fresh Step?

Me neither.

That is, until one Saturday morning, I found myself lounging in my partner's office, rhythmically tapping my keyboard as I awaited inspiration to strike. *What could I write about?*

Nick and I have three cats—brothers: Mars, Charlie, and Pascal. They were cuddled up next to me, as both their humans stared at glowing rectangles. Besides their fervent penchant to be glued to us, our kitties are also glued to each other.

So much so, they all share the same litter box—a behavior uncharacteristic of cats.

I glanced over to the huge black box in the corner—their toilet—and my eyes caught a bright container nearby. Bold, happy lettering exclaimed, *Extreme Hawaiian Aloha Cat Litter.* I noted the Fresh Step logo squarely in the middle.

Raising my eyebrow, I zoned out into a daydream.

Think, Bobby, think.

A man in a checkered button-down and khakis sits at his desk in a high rise on Broadway Street. What at first seems like another Tuesday at the Clorox headquarters in Oakland, CA, is actually an electric morning. His fingers dance above his keyboard, buzzing in anticipation of capturing the next big idea.

One of Clorox's subsidiaries, Fresh Step cat litter, is due for a new release.

Bobby is a marketer, responsible for breathing life into the brand. Now, he needs to create a cat litter scent—nay, an *experience*—that would fly off the shelves.

As his team reiterated in a recent planning meeting, the world of cat litter is enormous.

In the 1970s, the industry was a $200 million market that was growing at about 15 percent a year (Hyatt 1986).

In 2021, it had a $10.15 billion market cap. By 2028, the cat litter sector is expected to rise to $13.44 billion (*Cat Litter Products*, 2021). That's *billion*, baby.

You can imagine the stakes. For Bobby, the pressure is on—especially since he'd recently missed a week of work vacationing in Hawaii. It is crunch time. *What would he dream up next?*

He reviews his own company website. Currently in the Fresh Step rotation are five wholly distinct types, organized by price:

- Outstretch™ Concentrated Litter
- Scented Clumping Litter
- Unscented Clumping Litter
- Crystals
- Non-Clumping Litter

Bobby reflects on his childhood, visiting his grandparents out in the country and watching their outdoor toms paw the dirt in the yard after doing their business. He thinks about the two tabbies he begged his parents to get and how they always seemed to track the ground clay litter all over the orange carpet.

His eyes twinkle at the thought of his own orange tabby, Gus, currently sleeping in his apartment, and how delightful his home smells despite Gus' monstrous poops. It must be the genius clumping technology of his favorite, the *Clean Paws® Calm Rose and Chamomile Scented Litter*. Fresh Step brand, of course.

He smiles proudly to himself. *Oh, how far we've come.*

Yet now the clock is ticking and his design review meeting is in an hour.

Dammit! I've been staring at this glowing rectangle and there's still nothing on the screen! How can I make consumers give a shit about the next iteration of litter? How can I bring a new wave of delight to cat owners everywhere?

As if a cartoon lightbulb suddenly goes over his head, Bobby grabs his notebook and begins sketching furiously.

Inspired by island life and sweet scents he'd recently experienced in Honolulu, a new archetype starts to emerge.

He draws a tall, broad-shouldered man standing over a large box. He gives his character a name: Fabio.

Fabio is donned in a pristine white tank top, sweat-wicking shorts, and a sweatband on his forehead to keep his luscious blond locks at bay. His muscles ripple, his smile rivals the dazzle of the midday sun, and his voice—Bobby imagines his voice to be even more velvety than honey bourbon, which also happens to be his favorite drink.

So far, so good, Bobby smirks at his efforts. He continues to add to the sketch.

In Fabio's right hand is a small spade with rectangular holes in the base. Triumphantly, Fabio points this spade into the air, much like Poseidon and his trident, his face laced with an air of expectation.

Bobby's pencil moves madly as if a whole movie is playing out on paper.

In Fabio's world, everything suddenly jolts into stillness. A theatrical *dun-dun-dun* moment. Time slows to a crawl, seconds echo in the atmosphere. This god-like man takes his outstretched, shovel-wielding hand and drives it downward toward a mysterious box. Hardcore metal music plays in the background.

He plunges the shovel into the plastic container, every deltoid and bicep rippling as he scrapes the shovel along the bottom. Lifting his right hand slowly, the shovel now houses a golf-sized mass. Slate-gray crystals tumble through the spade's holes like the sands of time.

This paragon of a man, powerful and paramount, has just conquered the egregious implosion that is his cat's litter box.

Victory is his!

To reward this dynamic persona, Bobby adds one final detail to rule them all. With a flourish of graphite, Bobby bestows upon Fabio the insignia of triumph: a traditional Hawaiian lei. He can almost smell its sweetness through the paper.

This is it. This is the next big idea Fresh Step is looking for.

Extreme Hawaiian Aloha.

A rustle brought me back to reality. Our fluffiest cat, Mars, had just jumped in to use his personal toilet.

As Mars did his business, I thought about the imaginary marketer Bobby, beaming and proud of his efforts in naming the latest and greatest version of cat sand.

Prepare to be whisked away to a Hawaiian paradise, he'd kick off his design review. He'd point to the iconic mascot, the orange tabby on every Fresh Step box, chuffed because he's wearing a lei and contented smile. *While the breezes calm you with their dulcet aroma, rest assured our litter* just works. *It's extreme, after all!*

As the marketing team would clap and cheer, Bobby might think about that archetype he invented. This *Extreme Hawaiian Aloha* was the perfect litter for that imaginary, spade-wielding man donning a Hawaiian lei himself.

It struck me as highly amusing these *bags of dirt* portray entire personas. Whom do those creative marketing departments target? Is the ultimate consumer the cat or the cat owner?

While the answer is obvious, for we know only humans have the cognitive capacity to discern whether something is "Hawaiian-scented," what tickles me is the canyon-sized gap between what the cat cares about and what its owner cares about.

Until felines were domesticated, they spent their days frolicking out in deserts, plains, forests, and mountains, without an iota of thought to where they dumped their art. The only rules were for it to be away from predators and to establish territorial dominance.

When my childhood cat, Tangie, got lost for three weeks, he was not thinking about the conditions in which he peed and pooped. He went where he pleased—literally—until we found him in a drainage ditch. Even before the technologically advanced litter became available, domestic cats felt just dandy shitting in dirt.

But as humans began finding even more unique uses for their big and hungry prefrontal cortex—the brain region responsible for more advanced thought—professionals began dreaming up multiple ways to make more money and flood the consumer-driven economy with seemingly infinite options.

Many of them inane.

Like Extreme Hawaiian Aloha cat litter.

These huge corporations, like Clorox's Fresh Step, are selling not just cat litter to the masses, but moreover, a *concept*. We're guzzling it right up by the twenty-pound bag.

These marketers, including my imaginary friend Bobby, are clever enough to understand humans are silly enough to buy into a fusion of laundry detergent with clumping crystals, and to make a choice based on the *scent* that will mask their favorite feline's shit.

Oh, how far we've come.

Meanwhile, the cat is just as happy pooping in a box of dirt as it is in a state-of-the-art litter box with state-of-the-art litter. The pandering has not reached their little brains yet.

I sometimes wonder what's next for pet owners. We've already got contraptions that scoop cat shit themselves, without human touch. We've got toys that can entertain a kitty for hours via an automated feather on a string. We've got self-cleaning food and water bowls. What other *extreme* inventions will find their way into what we didn't know we wanted (or needed) but now *must* have?

As the seconds ticked on, I noticed Mars had finally finished his deed. Unlike his brothers, he did not bother pawing over his mess with those fancy crystals.

Strange.

I didn't smell any Hawaii or any alohas.

The smell that pervaded through the room was quite familiar to me now, thanks to years of cat ownership.

It was just...cat shit.

I got up off the bed, grabbed the now-purring Mars, and took him to another room.

"Mars," I said, looking into his emerald peepers.

"I'm gonna teach you how to use the human toilet."

"Mrreow!" he chirped happily, as we both left the Hawaiian paradise behind.

WAVING THROUGH TRAFFIC

———

There's something curiously effervescent about waving at people who don't expect it.

I grew up in one f the cities outside of Washington, DC, close enough to the nation's capital for a day trip, but far away enough to still hear crickets sing at night. Cookie-cutter houses whose walls almost kissed were sprinkled between ribbons of highway, with manicured lawns and rows of planted trees where forests once grew.

This was the image of suburbia: strip malls with restaurants for a million palates, most of them chains, nondescript office buildings keeping their insides clandestine with reflecting glass windows, and rivers of rush-hour traffic on every road, lane, strip of pavement.

It wasn't a bad place to grow up, for I had tremendous educational opportunities, but as a kid, I'd often find myself running, biking, and exploring to seek some pizzazz and excitement amid the backdrop of middle-class, American life.

As an only child, I relished the times I got to see people peopling. I observed them waiting impatiently in line for free samples at Costco, furrowing their brow at gas station prices while filling up monstrous SUVs, or scrolling on their phones while sitting in traffic. Catching people in their quotidian moments was more entertaining than a TV comedy about a group of average Joes and Janes. It was all so human to see.

Most of all, I relished the brief stint of connection with a stranger when we locked eyes and shared a small smile of recognition. I got to be in their world briefly, and they in mine.

Years ago, I was visiting my parents at my childhood home, nestled deep in the heart of suburban Northern Virginia. One unusually warm spring afternoon, I decided to go on a run through familiar landscapes, retracing memories of the multitude of miles over the last dozens-plus years.

As my feet pounded on an overpass across a major highway, the river of cars below roared over the music in my headphones. It was an engulfing onslaught of gray noise. Meanwhile, beneath me, individuals in their hermetically sealed boxes could just *barely* drown out the thunder of the traffic surrounding them.

Thousands of individuals, stuffed in cars kiss-distance apart, yet there was no connection.

It struck me as melancholic.

The bored, lonely, unenthused faces of drivers painted a bleak picture. What if there was a way to turn their frowns upside down?

Running along, I was nearing the end of the overpass and looking at the rapidly slithering snake below, each car a glistening scale rushing endlessly onward at sixty miles per hour. Suddenly, I stopped, mid-stride. Backpedaling, I retraced my steps to the middle of the overpass, gazing at the rushing cars, and began making rainbows with my hands.

Back and forth, back and forth, I waved.

About half a decade later, I found myself standing behind the fenced wall of an overpass spanning across the four-lane freeway known as the 101. I was just beginning my long afternoon run, an escape that came to be the antidote I craved in our lockdown-stricken world.

It was springtime in Los Angeles, and the air had an unusual crispness to it, smelling sweet before fire season destroyed the air quality and people's sinuses. The pandemic had been raging for over a year, and even then, even in the bustling metropolis of the City of Angels, there was a disquieting, empty feel. Not many people took to the streets. There were fewer cars than I'd ever seen in a city, both on east and west coasts.

I missed my friends and family, I missed going out to dive bars and intimate concerts, and most of all, I missed observing the mundane snippets of strangers' lives in coffee shops and other gathering places.

Even though the buildings differed from where I grew up, office parks replaced by rows of apartments in every style imaginable, the loneliness of a pandemic ghost town reminded me of the boredom of suburban streets.

Running gave me a chance to fill up my people-meter because there were bound to be at least a few adventurous souls milling about—definitely multitudes more than in my tiny apartment.

And so, there I was, looking at the trickle of cars below me zooming up and down the lanes at almost seventy-five miles per hour. Everything is faster in LA, including the fleeting moments of connection. I knew I needed to make myself seen.

I raised both hands and back and forth, back and forth, I waved.

How do we connect with strangers?

We do it with whimsy. We do it by tweaking the social norms we may feel confined to. We do it by breaking the monotony of an afternoon commute.

As I stood there on that bridge overlooking the freeway with LA's mountains as a glorious backdrop, I kept helicoptering my arms. I felt like I was flying, like a delicious joy bubbled up and out through my body and filled me with fizzy buoyancy.

The majority of faces behind windshields kept their steely stare on the pavement ahead. However, the select few who caught my wild waving flashed a hint of white: smiles. Those same bodies, jolted by curiosity, waved back.

This was *joy*.

Here were strangers, unknowingly thrust into the same space and time of existence by sheer chance in one of the most mundane activities—commuting—and connected over a universal symbol of *hello*.

Hello, new friend. It's nice to meet you, if only for a split second.

As worlds intersected over and over for mere moments, I couldn't help but smile wider and wider. Grinning turned into laughter turned into pure, unadulterated elation. I was floating, effervescent, lifted by the smiles of strangers below. The locked-down city suddenly didn't feel so lonely.

Energized by these microdoses of connection, I restarted my run, waving madly behind me at the traffic below. As the honks receded, I ran through a familiar memory from years prior. There, standing on the overpass in suburban Northern Virginia, I, too, recalled feeling a little less alone.

How many times do we pass up an opportunity to connect with another human being, especially a stranger, just for the hell of it? To look into their eyes as they pass by, instead of looking away? To really see them in a snapshot of their everyday moments, because those moments are everything anyone's really got?

When our initial, ingrained impulse is to *stay in our lanes*, perhaps it's time to look up, and wave.

ON FINDING JOY WHEN YOU'RE TIRED OF LOOKING

———

Yesterday, I was skipping stones and laughing at crabs on the beach in sheer delight.

Today, I am sobbing softly to myself because it's already 8:37 p.m. and I still haven't worked out or eaten dinner.

I can't find a concrete reason to be matching the immense, slate-gray smear of clouds outside. I suppose it started when I woke up early enough to have a quiet, slow morning to myself before work, but ended up being sucked back into the warmth of a human and three cats for forty minutes instead.

Then, feeling rushed, just moments before I was due to hop on a Zoom call with my book editor, I dropped my brand-new contact, left eye, somewhere on the pink-and-white-tiled bathroom floor.

One eye was in focus, the other a blur of colors sans shapes.

Fuck it, I thought. *I'll just wear my glasses with the way-out-dated prescription.*

And so, the day unfolded.

First up, I had to mock-present a two-hour-long workshop I'd just learned a few days prior, and realized I was ill-prepared. My job involves guiding managers and executives through tailored, interactive learning experiences. To be successful, we need to have our content, presentation, and audience engagement on point, especially since we're currently teaching virtually. If you thought keeping attention spans of busy adults standing at, well, attention, for two hours *in person* was hard enough, try doing it through a thirteen-inch screen.

And I wasn't doing so well with this new material. I could feel heat rising in my face during the run-though with my proctor, knowing I needed to pass it to teach.

I thought back to the beach I was at the day prior, watching the waves roll in and crash from a safe distance on the rocks. Now, I felt like I was being towed underwater.

My kind proctor gave me a conditional pass on the mock with the expectation I practice and practice and practice.

Afterward, I practiced being mopey instead.

The sun didn't come out for the rest of the day, but another celestial object *did* appear. In the mirror, I noticed a zit the size of Pluto had made its home on my face.

Let me try to pop it to make it go away, I thought.

I thought wrong.

It now represented Saturn, with its red, circular rings from my poking and prodding. What didn't help was the pink frame of my old glasses accentuating the pink on my cheek. Throughout the day, I kept noticing how I could only see within the boundaries of my frames, and any time I'd look up or to the side, all I would see was blurriness.

This gave me a sort of tunnel vision that seemed to highlight the low-grade ennui of the day.

By the time evening rolled around, I was exhausted by my ten-hour workday, extended because I ran through the workshop several more times with my patient partner in hopes of mastering it before the imminent deadline. Even after those repetitions, I came away with the daunting realization I needed to practice, practice, practice some more. My brain was fried.

There *had* to be a way to turn this ship around.

Naturally, I resorted to putting off the one thing I knew was an instant pick-me-up: a workout.

A phenomenon has recently been making headlines called "revenge bedtime procrastination." It's where a person deliberately stays up late, usually scrolling on their phone or doing some other mind-numbing task in an attempt to feel a morsel of control over their time, because they perceive they *didn't* have that control during the day (Liang 2020).

And even though it wasn't bedtime, I found myself switching through scrolling on Reddit, Facebook, and Instagram, as if the faster I could inhale online junk, the better I would feel.

I felt even worse.

I knew my personal inbox was overflowing with unanswered emails. Seventeen new text messages popped up over the course of the day, even though I was proud of answering a huge majority of them from the past month just this morning.

I couldn't even make space to think about the LinkedIn, WhatsApp, and Messenger alerts all vying for replies, not to mention book deadlines, an upcoming trip to see family, and the existential crisis three-quarters of the year had seemingly evaporated, and I felt I had almost nothing to show for it.

Just your standard Monday, right?

Yet I was still glued to the couch in a state of paralysis.

These thought patterns carried me to almost nine in the evening, compounded by the knowledge I needed to be up in ten hours to be fresh for a long day of work—again.

But wait, wasn't I writing a book on finding joy?

It struck me as ironic the very subject I was devoting months to capture after a lifetime of seamless execution was now the very thing that seemed so unattainable. For all I knew, today was an ordinary day where nothing bad happened, yet I felt like a deflated balloon. My usual zest was zapped.

So why wasn't I practicing my own deeply rooted belief to look for joy in plain sight?

I took off my glasses, rubbing the spots on the bridge of my nose where the plastic made angry indents.

Hmm. My tunnel vision was gone.

Even though everything, uniformly, was now out of focus, I decided this was my opportunity to switch contexts and *re*focus. If I was going to spring into action, I needed to first set my mind.

A cat meme on Reddit jolted me out of doom-scrolling, and I thought back to the kitties on my bed this morning. How did I get so lucky to wake up every day next to my favorite person *and* my three favorite felines? And that, despite how challenging my job was, I had the opportunity to take a break to travel for a whole week to see my family and *their* cat back east? And how do I *get* the chance to splash like a kid in tide pools on weekends, even if it comes with the occasional pimple?

Slapping my knees, I shook myself out of my stupor and told myself *C'mon, let's go.*

And go I did. My favorite fitness app guided me through a twenty-minute cardio dance workout and a refreshing yoga stretch. In all the squats, lunges, and deep breathing, I remembered the connection to my own body. Heels and calves, elbows, and wrists twisted in all directions, regaining blood flow.

I regained awareness of my limbs.

As I lay on the mat, I recalled the sea crabs I'd seen scuttling across the moss-covered rocks by the beach. How easily they shuffled left and right, how effortlessly they scaled vertical rock walls and wedged themselves into the tiniest crevasses. It was like they were born to live within their bodies.

We as humans are born to live in our bodies, too. We're designed to move our vessels and feel the groundedness beneath our feet. However, what we—or at least I, today—felt was the gusty whirlwind of thoughts, floating high above any center. I was living in the storms of the *have-to*s and *should*s within my mind.

After my "namaste," I got up, took a quick shower, and caught my own smile in the mirror.

Huh. The dark clouds were gone. Despite the small pinprick of pink—now back to Pluto's size—my skin glowed. It was only a quarter past nine. I had a whole hour or two until I needed to wind down to sleep.

I buzzed with renewed energy.

As I grabbed my laptop to sit down and write, I kept coming back to the little creatures by the seashore. Those crabs don't have bad days. They open their beady eyes, pluck some moss with their pincers, wrestle with one another, and dance about. In the middle of a side scuttle, a big wave comes and pummels them against the rock. They hang on for dear life because that is what they know how to do.

They live within their bodies.

And we, with our fancy brains and developed prefrontal cortices, find ways to mope around without due cause. This complex gray mass behind our skull has a conniving ability to let perception cloud our judgment, much like my own dark cumulonimbus storm on this particular day. Nothing is wrong, yet everything feels off, and we wallow in our vices.

But unlike those crabs, whose goal is to survive the pummeling of the ocean, we get a *choice* in how we see the pummeling waves of our gloomier days. Thanks to our big, beautiful, messy brains, we can remember we don't *have* to cross things off our to-do lists; we *get* to. We can reframe a lost contact as a lesson to see through the fuzzy tunnel vision. Recall our bodies can dance too.

Precisely in those moments when the world is swirling, we have the ultimate power to *still* find the joy.

As I answered the call of my beckoning bed, I reflected on the preceding sixteen hours. Work and zits and endless messages were my versions of constant waves.

I could either get swept in the undertow or let my body swim. Let my body remember it can move, dance, and choose to do things that bubble up in joy. And when those waves come crashing over, I can call on my brain to remind me stormy skies produce the most brilliant azure spread.

And so I swam into the ocean of dreams, hoping to dance with crabs in sheer delight.

WASHING DISHES

———

"Can't we *please* just stop and get a burger?" I pleaded.

My mother swiveled from her passenger seat and looked at me sternly.

"Katya, listen to yourself. We have cabbage and fish at home. Let's cook something really quickly when we arrive. It'll take twenty minutes: I'll throw the tilapia in the oven, and you make the salad and set the table."

As immigrants from the fractured former Soviet Union, my family didn't really have much, so a lot of normally automated or outsourced tasks were done by hand. *Why would we pay for things with money we didn't have, when we could simply do it ourselves?*

For example, I don't recall a single instance we ordered in food and can count on *one* hand the number of times we went out to eat. Even during eight-hour road trips home from vacation, hungry and tired in our cramped car, my begging for fast food went unfulfilled.

After all, we could cook food at home.

One summer day in our first year in America, my enterprising mother and my seven-year-old self donned yellow paper crowns and named ourselves queens of the kitchen. We were going to spend all day making pizza.

We prepared all our own ingredients and toppings from scratch and kneaded the dough for seemingly hours. Bags of flour, sugar, and yeast would last us months compared to the price of a single delivery order. Back then, I thought I knew the epitome of luxury: being able to recreate the pizza I saw in Domino's television commercials in our tiny one-bedroom apartment.

When we moved into a townhome a few years later, I was designated as the cleaner of our three-story house. Every weekend, that meant wiping and scrubbing all three bathrooms top-down, and inching on hands and knees with a rag to make sure the hundreds of square feet of wooden floors sparkled.

And oh, they *had* to sparkle—or else. No, a Swiffer wouldn't do. Elbow grease was the best cleaner.

"Tree, tree, tree," my mom would command in Russian.

You'd think the word for "scrub" repeated over and over would conjure up an image of a calming forest dense with lovely trees to ease the eyes. Instead, I saw my own annoyed reflection in the elbow-grease-shined hardwood floors.

Because I was the chore-master, this also meant I did all the dishes. All of them, all three meals, all the time. Normally, this would not be a big deal, but my mother also loved to cook, and damn well, too. You can imagine the glass and ceramic and metal mountain ranges sprouting in the sink several times a day.

I felt like a mountaineer, delicately dancing up the cup-and-plate Himalayas, ensuring no avalanche occurred from sudden movement. What made this even more complicated was we didn't have a dishwasher.

Oh, woe is me, having to wash all the dishes by hand; go cry me a river.

I know, I know; there are other things to groan about. But, when you're a kid and you want to go play, or need to complete homework, or desire to nonchalantly skip from the dinner table and *do something, anything, else*—and you can't—things got sticky.

See, I loathed doing dishes. After fifteen minutes of scrubbing, my back would start to hurt. A slight nagging would turn into a full-on, persistent ache, no matter how I repositioned my feet or wiggled my spine. This pain started when I was a teenager, thanks to all the intense tumbling on a razor-thin mat during high school gymnastics.

Despite my pleas and cries, my mother wouldn't have any of it.

"Ay, davay, delai!"

"You better do it!" she would scold, maternal wrath coming through with vigor in our mother tongue.

All I wanted was to be done.

To stop scrubbing the pile of dishes, to dry my hands from the soapy suds, to be anywhere but the kitchen, grumbling to myself about all the things I'd rather be doing. All I wanted was to be somewhere else, to do something else.

Fast-forward a few decades to early spring. It is morning, the kind that feels like a stolen sliver of time, before the rest of the world is up. My only companion is the sun, yawning and stretching its long rays, ready to warm up the day.

Water for the coffee is boiling, and just a few feet away is a dance performance. I'm scrubbing my plates from last night and letting my hands sashay in the faucet's waterfall. I am the conductor, orchestrating a circular ballet of the sponge on the ceramic stage, and the occasional quickstep for those caked-on food particles hanging on for dear life.

Today, the water feels heavenly: a steady stream of warmth, enough to radiate its heat down to my cold, bare feet, but cool enough to be a balm of relief against the rough sponge.

As I wash the dishes, I also notice what is happening inside. In my mind's eye, I observe myself drifting on a wooden boat down a lazy river. I think about the inviting water, the curves of the cups, and how the rivulets rush down the sheer face of a vertical plate en route to the drying rack.

I don't think about much else. I don't think about my to-do list for the day, the week, the year, the millions of notifications on my phone since last night, how I need to work and run and work some more.

I find I am suspended in a limbo of space and time.

While my hands are doing, my mind is being.

These five or ten morning minutes are my insulation against the world's assault of announcements, needs, pings—information overload I subject myself to.

And so I let my mind wander, languidly watching thoughts come and go. In with a swish of the sponge, out with the faucet's waterfall.

This is meditation, isn't it? To be so fully present, to enjoy each singular moment as it arises—despite gnarly roots of the past and anxious tendrils of the future. Not even the mundane task of washing the dishes can sway me from this comfort.

After all, as Buddhist monk and "father of mindfulness" Thich Nhat Hanh said, "If I am incapable of washing dishes joyfully, if I want to finish them quickly so I can go and have dessert or a cup of tea, I will be equally incapable of enjoying my dessert or my tea when I finally have them" (Nhat Hanh 2019).

And so I smile to myself at the dichotomy of experience between my childhood and my present. How, as a kid, all I wanted was for this chore to be done. And how now, as an adult, I'm finding myself leaning into it, loving the space of soapy suds and thoughts.

I reflect on my recent move into a new home with my partner. How our house and stage in life affords us to have all the amenities—and nights of Domino's pizza—we could ever want.

We even have a Swiffer, yet I insist on scrubbing those stubborn spots on our kitchen floor by hand.

A little elbow grease never hurt.

And even though we now have a dishwasher for the first time in my adult life—at the insistence of my partner who also hates washing dishes—I still wash my own plates by hand.

I roll out of bed in the morning, put the coffee on, albeit with a fancier machine than my now unused French press, and push up my pajama sleeves on those chilly autumn mornings. Then, I plunge into the lukewarm water and drift into a timeless space, hands in tango with the plates, the cups, and the spoons.

I have nowhere else to be but here, nothing else to do but wash dishes, if only for these five meditative minutes, and that is perfectly fine with me.

GROUNDED IN TIME

———

My mother swirls what's left of her Turkish coffee and tips her cup to show me the mud.

On the last day of a weeklong visit to my parents in Virginia last fall, my mom and I steal a moment on the balcony for a cuppa before my father and my partner Nick get ready for family brunch.

I'm on my third serving, since these cups and saucers are tiny and I just want more caffeine to wake up. Good thing the finely ground beans taste extra strong this morning.

"Do you know how to read coffee grounds?" she asks with a playful twinkle in her eye.

"Hmm, that looks like a cat's face," I joke, seeing nothing besides splotches of brown-black sludge in indeterminate forms.

My mother, seemingly ageless in her sixty years, with wrinkles nearly invisible from where I'm sitting across the table on the balcony of my childhood home, looks down into the small, white and pearlescent, porcelain cup.

She stares into it for a long beat, and I observe her against the backdrop of green trees tinged with orange and yellow leaves in mid-autumn. A swirl of freshness reaches our nostrils, wind invigorated from last night's rain, and makes a pleasant contrast to the strong coffee.

She is peaceful, perhaps a tad contemplative, and her mood reflects the moment. I try to imagine what she's imagining and draw a blank. It's fascinating trying to unpack what images dance and sing in a loved one's head, especially one who gave me the ability to see through the sludge.

"I think it looks like a clock. See the circle and the two hands there?" she says.

I look back in her cup and think about time and its scarcity.

Growing up, I remember grumbling in slight annoyance when my mother would insist on bringing out the fancy china for a simple morning coffee.

"Ugh, but Mom, we have regular mugs instead! The fancy cups are so high up on the shelf," my sixteen-year-old self would complain.

Perhaps it was my resist-anything-my-parents-liked phase—being a teenager—but I really didn't understand why my mother made such a big deal about taking extra time to set an entire feast of a table just for coffee. She'd pepper the spread with homemade raspberry jams and those fancy, tiny spoons, perhaps a basket of warmed-up croissants, and a plate of cheese and dried fruits.

Why all the formality around something we drank every day?

The way that coffee operated in my world was a matter of pragmatism. I started making it a part of my routine in college to keep up with the demand of school and work, and I never really stopped. I'd pour myself a mug before my 8 a.m. class and stop at the local campus coffee shop to catch an afternoon break to replenish my caffeine reserves.

During those early mornings, shitty instant coffee was my daily staple. I wonder why on earth I tolerated the burnt taste of the dissolving crystals. And yet, I downed every last drop.

I think about all the cafes I frequented in my college town. A first date at Milli. A breakup at Hot Cakes. Countless hours in Java Java hunched over my undergraduate thesis, only to boomerang back to the very same spot a few years later to compose papers for grad school. Those local shops were my home to write and to sip. I'd finish a cup or two well before I'd finish my work for that afternoon and push the saucer away so I could focus.

Concentrating on my laptop screen, I didn't really pause to search for any patterns at the bottoms of my cups.

A few years after I graduated from university and left my first job in consulting, I returned to work full-time in that picturesque college town nestled between the Blue Ridge Mountains. Almost every Friday and Saturday for two years, I'd drive two and a half hours to in-person graduate school classes in Washington, DC. Luckily, my parents lived close enough to campus and let me sleep in my childhood bedroom between or after classes.

On late Sunday mornings, I'd stumble out of my tiny bedroom, head heavy with the weekend's learnings and the prior week's work. My routine was to grab a quick bite with my family before making the long drive back to my mountain home before the next work week began.

"Katya, go grab the little cups and saucers." My mom, already awake and bustling for a few hours, was referring to that fancy china set she so loved.

The set consisted of six tiny cups, six saucers, a milk jug, a lidded sugar bowl, and a tall coffee server. Each of those items was milky white with a gold rim and boasted pearlescent puddles on the sides, as if shimmering soap bubbles burst onto the porcelain surface. Golden line designs on the rainbow glint reminded me of phoenix wings.

This set has lived in our cupboards my entire life, having made its way gingerly across the world when we emigrated from Uzbekistan to the United States when I was a kid.

The pieces were nearly flawless after all these decades—thanks to the level of delicate handling my mother required.

I learned the china set was a gift from my maternal grand-mother. She'd bought it almost forty years ago and gave it to my parents when they got married. It became a family heirloom.

"But see here, on the bottom?" My mom stuck the cup under my nose for closer inspection during one of those Sunday brunches. We were sipping in the present while reflecting on the past.

"This is the mark of quality, that this was fine craftsmanship."

I noticed a red symbol and next to it the letters "CCCP," indi-cating its origin from the former Soviet Union. This set was a piece of history creating even more memories through a deliberate pause in time.

During grad school, I'd picked up the habit of chugging six-teen ounces of Dunkin's iced coffee a few times a month while always on the go—in the car, on a walk, during work—any-where but the present moment. My mom, on the other hand, would architect our coffee time to be almost painfully slow.

After setting the fine cups on their fine saucers, she'd pour us the delicious, black liquid to only about two-thirds full. After pointing to the creamer and some honey nearby, she'd sit back in her chair, content.

"Mmm," my mother would intonate, smacking her lips gently together after a tiny yet leisurely sip. "Taste it on just the tip of your tongue; you don't need to take a big gulp."

She'd smile and close her eyes to savor.

This slow-sipping practice originated from our cultural immersion living in Uzbekistan. As in many Asian countries, it was tradition to sit around the table with family and friends for prolonged meals. The tradition I grew up with was drinking *chai*: Russian for tea, made with plain green or black leaves and piping-hot water.

We carried this practice over to America. After a hearty dinner, my mom and I would walk around the neighborhood to give our bellies a chance to make space for what was coming. Then, back home, she'd ask me to grab the *pialki*—chai cups—for tea. Just tea, rarely any dessert.

Of course, if we had no plans for that evening, the fancy china would make its presence. It was a different set than the coffee china cups. However, the tea set was still white with a golden rim on the sides. I guess fanciness has a consistent design.

Throughout the next hour, we'd sit around the table, drinking our plain tea from our *pialki*, tasting, smelling, smiling.

"See, we are carrying on the tradition of tea drinkers!" my father would quip holding the teapot.

I'd look into my cup and see it was only about two-thirds full. After a few years of living in the American mindset of "bigger is better," it would slightly bug me as a kid our cups were never filled to the brim.

Why not just pour all ten or twelve or however many ounces to the lip of the cup? *Fewer refills, more tea.*

I finally learned the reason for this practice when Nick and I sat through a few tea times during our visit back home.

"You know, pouring a cup about halfway is a sign of respect for the drinker," my father started, looking at Nick, again holding his beloved teapot, also an original piece of china from our family. "Since the tea is hot, you want to pour it *just so*, so your guest does not burn his mouth."

"And," he said with a playful wink, "it keeps tea and conversations flowing!"

During those tea times as a kid, I'd be itching to be finished so I could go do my homework or play. Even on this past trip home as a well-seasoned adult, I'd make eyes with Nick across the table to signal we should wrap up and head to our next engagement, even if it was upstairs to take a break from all the eating and drinking with our bellies sorely full. There was always somewhere else to be.

That final morning on the balcony proved to be no different. I pour my fourth Turkish coffee cup, desperately waiting for the caffeine to kick in, and calculate how much time we have left before catching our flight back to Los Angeles.

My mom looks at me as if to say *slow down*. She leans her head back against the balcony chair, corners of her mouth upturned in satisfaction.

Mirroring her, I set my little saucer down and do the same.

A few hours later, Nick and I wait among the crowd of rushed passengers eager to get on their flight. All around me, it seems like every fifth person is clutching a coffee cup, even though the afternoon hours are already waning. *Take a gulp, grab your luggage, hop on the plane.*

We are a nation hooked on caffeine, jonesing for that quick fix, that rapid burst of energy. We guzzle large lattes from Starbucks, Dunkin', Peets, our local coffee shop down the street. *Bigger is better,* we think, *and we'd like that to go, please.*

As I'm sitting at the gate waiting for our boarding group to be called, I finally feel like I've paused as the rest of the airport world hurtles by.

Where have I tasted this pause before?

In my mind's eye, I paint a picture of the coffee grounds at the bottom of a tiny, porcelain cup. The moment is still, wind gently rustling tree leaves, making the wispy tendrils from the hot coffee dance above my cup. I am sitting on the balcony of my childhood home, sipping on homemade coffee at an impossibly slow pace.

Perhaps it's not even about the coffee at all.

Nor the tea, nor the fancy china sets.

In my mother's insistence on making sure we use the nice cups, perhaps she's insisting we drink in the moment.

All those times using those pearlescent, porcelain cups, passed down from her mother, was her way of slowing down the inevitable rush of the outside world.

Was I always too busy to notice this deliberate pause?

I look up at the screen by the airport gate and catch the digital display turn from 4:59 to 5:00. And, just like that, our boarding group is called. We grab our luggage to file in line for the plane.

As I stand, an image flashes in my head from earlier this morning. It's my mother's porcelain cup, with the sludgy coffee grounds in the shape of a clock, a moment when time stood still.

THE SOUND OF SILENCE

Beep. Beep. Beep. Beep.

It is trash day. I'm sitting on a balcony in the Hollywood Hills, surrounded by dark greens and grating sounds.

The moan of the trash truck reminds me of a cow with a head cold, mooing its way up and down the sinuous streets of this neighborhood.

It's fascinating to me the iconic—and annoying—back-up beeper is instantly recognizable. If an alien were to land anywhere in America, it would immediately learn that unmistakable beeping is synonymous with large objects moving in backward directions.

For some reason—whether it's the contrast of the silence in the empty apartment I'm house-sitting for, or a morbid curiosity for things that drive most people up the wall—I fall into a bit of a rabbit hole researching trash trucks.

As the truck beeps in the background, I learn most back-up beepers produce sounds in the 1,000-1,200-hertz range, which is absolutely meaningless to any non-musician and me. I just know that feels like a large, strident number.

To try mapping it on a musical scale, I take a guess and pull up the YouTube search bar: "B flat note." The first result that pops up is a steady sound, a bit nasally, but not quite matched with the truck I hear in the distance.

My search history looks like this:
- 1000-hertz tuning
- What sound does a trash truck make
- Back-up truck note
- 1000 hertz is what note

Cross-referencing several university research pages, I approximate that 1,000 hertz rests between a B5 and C6 note (Botros 2001; Suits 1998). This still tells me slightly more than nothing but feels like I'm making progress because I've nailed down a concrete space on the musical scale.

I pat myself on the back for approximating my initial B-flat-note guess as the primary signal of trash day.

As the truck recedes into the soundscape, I shift my focus to the hum about two football fields away. A particular yet familiar song catches my ear: the song of car tires shushing lullabies to the asphalt, with the occasional percussive fart of a sports car accelerator, prompting the wheels to sing louder.

This is the eternal sound of the 101.

Built almost a whole century ago in 1926, the north-south US freeway connects the western coastal states of Washington, Oregon, and California. It runs across the Golden Gate Bridge, stretches over the Columbia River, and is made up of over 1,500 miles of road (Cooper 1999).

During my first two years in Los Angeles, the 101 also became a consistent white-noise soundtrack humming in the background of everyday life.

It is a river of cars, similar to a river carrying fish and insects. At first listen, it is a constant, fuzzy, TV-static rush. The more you listen, though, the more nuance you pick up.

You hear the semis as deep trombones. Small cars as zaggy clarinet sneezes. Cars with busted mufflers as screaming cellos. The occasional trumpet of horns signaling the perceived idiocy of drivers traveling at—seemingly—the speed of sound.

The river of traffic has a specific sound signature—just like the trash truck backing up into my audio perception. Suddenly, a different sound pierces my awareness. I hear a singular, cerulean…

…bird call.

Cheeeeerp! CheeeEEEeeerp!

It just *sounds* blue. Like a radiant, pinpricked pluck of azure gliding in parabolically from one mountain face to its neighbor.

And again, only this time it's:

Chi-chi-chi-chi-chi!

Consistent. Steady. A heartbeat.

These sounds pierce empty dampness. I am completely blanketed by a silver mist rolling high across mountain tops as I stand as a tiny dot on a large peak. Thirty feet in any direction: *nothing.*

Below me is the cool, dusty-yellow ground. I pretend I am a giantess stomping on a late-summer field of wheat, high up enough where even the colors begin to blend.

I am surrounded by dark greens on three sides, up in the neck of a canyon, on my way down from a strenuous summit. As the giantess, I imagine picking up a paintbrush and dipping it into earthy hues. The pigment on my brush weighs wet, heavy, in browns and yellows and greens of every shade. Taking my hand up to my eye, I slowly sweep the horizon with my imaginary landscape, bringing it to life.

I pause my hike and try to still my breath. My heart pounds in my ears, and I want to hear the *chi-chi-chi-chi-chi* bird cry again, to hear if my human heartbeat is syncopated or synchronized with birdsong. In three minutes of stillness, six discrete bird species sing their mating call.

Because of the fog, not only is the city below invisible to me, but its sharp city sounds also lose their spikes. What I *don't* hear is silence, because silence is the absence of sound.

No, instead, it is a steady hum, a low, rushing rumble from the underbelly of mountain peaks.

Remember when, as a kid on your annual family beach vacation, your parents handed you a sizable conch shell from the shore and motioned to put it up to your ear? How the sea seemed to swell in your left ear, with an incessant *shh* sound?

The groan beneath the mountain peaks sounds just like that, in true surround-sound fashion. You are inside the shell and the muffled hum is squeezing you from every angle, constant.

It sounds just like the 101.

I am both comforted and unsettled I can straddle two worlds at once: the occasional cheery chirp from mating birds and the dulled city below.

It's a privilege, hearing two distinct environments at the same time, precisely because they are so discordantly opposed. Nature does not know car horns; and people zipping around in cars do not pause long enough to catch the flutter of a hummingbird's wing—because they can't. The birds are drowned out.

It's also claustrophobic, hearing the muted cityscape without being able to attribute it to any visual cause. I can't discern the river of traffic, with its honking semis, broken sports car mufflers, and tires singing their ever-louder lullabies. It's like living in a giant shell: hearing the roar but not being able to see much beyond your imagination.

I wonder what it would sound like for there to be absolute....

...silence.

We're lying on our backs supported by the roof of the Jeep, with a thin layer of blankets under our sweatshirts.

It's mid-August. Friday the thirteenth, with a chill in the air laced not with superstition, but rather with the frosty bite of a Southern California desert night. It is also a perfectly notable date to watch the sky cry fire.

My partner Nick and I are deep, deep into the Angeles National Forest, miles up the wandering thirty-five-miles-per-hour-limit road, far past the point cell reception cuts out. We are tethered to nothing, except the hopeful longing of our eyes married to the dark heavens.

We drive out here past midnight, way past bedtime, to observe our biennial meteor shower. Tonight's flavor are the Perseids, originating from the constellation Perseus, mythologized as Zeus' son and slayer of the Gorgon Medusa, with her head of hissing snakes.

We are united by body heat, with protruding, skyward noses the only bits of flesh exposed enough to get a hint of night chill.

Every few minutes sails a shimmering ribbon across the night sky, and I yell with delight. "Woah! Did you see that one? Massive!"

I wish I could hear the roar of the shooting stars as they fall toward Earth, but instead of a 132,000-miles-per-hour fire, all I hear is...nothing.

There is absolute silence, almost like what it might feel like to exist in a vacuum. I swear I hear my blood course through my veins and my organs jiggle inside.

It's the kind of silence that's loud. A strident, thunderous nothingness, similar to the afterimage effect of its sister sense, sight. You know when you stare at a particular color against a light background for a minute and look away?

What do you see?

The opposite color. Reds turn into greens, blues turn into oranges, purples to yellows.

Here, in the heart of the forest, I hear such a lack of traffic, of honking, of the city screaming its lungs hoarse, the silence is deafening.

As my eyes acclimate to white freckles of the dark-skinned sky, my eardrums, too, begin to vibrate with passing murmurs.

A bat chitters overhead, with its giggly flap of wings forming an aural parabola above us. The crickets begin to emerge into my awareness as well.

Reee! Reee! Reee! Reee! Steady. Constant.

My body melts into the stillness, and I focus on the distinct sounds of nature's slumber. She's not sleeping at all but conducting an orchestral arrangement of dozens of species whose turn it is to cry from their soapbox.

Besides the occasional car zooming by, there is not one man-made disturbance in the ambience. I think about Perseus up there in the sky, sending shooting stars from his sword, slashing away at Medusa's dozen snakes. I liken the snakes' hissing to the grating city soundscape.

Perhaps Perseus' Perseids drew us out into the silence to escape.

As we watch the periodic meteors fly overhead, I realize I don't miss the sound of the city at all.

There is a theory in biology called the acoustic niche hypothesis, developed by musician and ecology researcher Bernie Krause and his colleague Stuart Gage. It posits in wild ecosystems, species carve out their own frequencies and pitches at which they vocalize (Spiegel, Rosin, and Wendle 2020).

To understand the importance of this, we must first clarify two terms: geophony and biophony.

Geophony (from the Greek prefix *geo* meaning earth, and *phon* meaning sound) refers to the soundscape created by earthly phenomena. Think the whoosh of wind, the shushing of a river, the boom of thunder.

Biophony (this time from the Greek prefix *bio* meaning life) describes the sounds made by any species able to produce a sound. Birds, cats, frogs, rattlesnakes; the list is truly endless.

What's beautiful is scientists have been able to measure the flavor of biophony amid the geophony. Through highly calibrated instruments, they are able to detect the frequencies of many species even when they're vocalizing all at once.

Why? This is where the acoustic niche hypothesis comes into play. Let's break down what the two components are and see what's in a name.

Acoustic means relating to sound. And *niche* is a specialized place to thrive in optimal conditions or environments.

So, the theory tells us biophony—or sounds from any vocalizing creature—exists at the perfect place for each species.

Namely, any animal within a particular ecosystem has evolved to yell into the world at a distinct frequency and pitch to not get in each other's way.

Altogether, their sounds *fit* like an aural jigsaw puzzle.

Their sounds *fit* and *play together* like an orchestra.

We are surrounded by expert composers, the Beethovens and Mozarts of the animal kingdom. Only they didn't need years of practice to hone their scores. Instead, their music comes from within, passed down through thousands of generations of composers before them.

As *Invisibilia* podcast host Abby Wendle says, "Improbable as it sounds, it makes a kind of beautiful intuitive sense. Many creatures need to hear and be heard to find food, water, mates. And it's best to do that without wasting energy. So, they evolved over millions and millions of years to all make sounds together but without interrupting each other. It's like evolution actually forged a sonic civility."

So, when we hear the arc of six different bird calls on top of a foggy mountain, we hear the six distinct, parallel songs, with each artist striving to leave their mark.

However, we as humans, leave our own mark, too.

This is where anthrophony enters the scene.

Anthro is the Greek prefix for *people*, and anthrophony covers all the meaningful and meaningless sounds our kind produce. Think of actual symphonies and orchestras, caterwauling, whispering, and general farting about. Think, also, of the droning hums of highways crisscrossing every plain, forest, mountain range in the world. Think of the 101.

We live in an unstill world, and this is a problem for the ecosystems in those plains, forests, mountain ranges.

Researchers discovered when environments are encroached upon by the weeds of sound—anthrophony—the animals that were once in sync and singing to their own drumbeat start playing out of tune.

For example, there is a species of frog that all sing at the same time, at the same frequency. They do this as a defense mechanism, to *sound* bigger and more menacing to predators. However, when large military jets began flying over their habitat, the frogs would lose their place on their sheet music and syncopate instead of synchronize. They became particularly vulnerable to swooping predators from the skies.

In time, the frog population—and other species—diminished or disappeared completely as a result of our chaotic symphonies.

And so, the original orchestras break down, falling into disarray. Because of our horns, the horns of the animal world die off. Because of the beeping of our trash trucks, the cheeping of the winged creatures becomes muted, notes crumbling from the musical staff like dead bits of rock and ice racing down toward Earth.

We as a species have carved out the largest acoustic niche possible, drowning out all the other music-makers in the world. I am reminded of this as the B5 beep swings back down my street, constant, grating, and shouting over the blue jays who are just trying to sing.

How can we mollify the effects of the conch shell of human creation?

To be clear, we, too, expel beauty through our symphonies. Over the summer, I got the tremendous opportunity to hear and see the Los Angeles Philharmonic play alongside Christina Aguilera.

The vibrations from clarinets, drums, violas, vocal cords made every body in the 17,500-person stadium quiver. I wondered what goosebumps would sound like.

But I'm more concerned with the noise from freeways, metal birds, and the persistent hum of city life that sometimes feels like a metallic ocean. *How can we reduce our acoustic footprint that way?*

I think the answer lies in seeking a different kind of sound.

Silence.

It's putting down the conch shell from our ear and sitting atop mountains and listening to the songs sung effortlessly, all around us, without machines, without instruments.

It's stealing a few moments from each day, for yourself, to pause as creators and join an audience of listeners.

It's noticing that hummingbird whiz by your head. That bee you'd normally swat away. The lively dance of leaves in an autumn breeze.

I am sitting in a park, now four football fields removed from the 101, yet I still hear the distant river of cars and the generators behind the apartment buildings. However, I'm finding that, after minutes of acclimation, my ears and brain have a powerful sensitivity to focus on the chitter of the crow perched on the fern tree behind me, the patter of zippy hummingbird wings to my left, and the rustle of the palm tree fronds up ahead.

I smile in stillness—in silence.

I keep smiling through a truck's faint B5 backup beeper, eyes closed, the giantess in me straddling the biophonic and anthrophonic worlds all around.

SEWING AND SOWING

———

I shut the red front gate of my quadplex apartment building and step into a Tuesday.

The air is ripe with anticipation of the workday ahead. Its honeyed fragrance—emanating from those yellow-and-white plumeria flowers—whisks you away to the finest Parisian perfume shop.

The shores of the LA river of traffic have not yet overflowed; it's too early for the snarl of smog. I inhale freshness and autumn. My lungs dance at their fulfillment.

Down the steps and onto the sidewalk below, I linger for a moment. My feet, clad in orange Chacos sandals, kiss the cement, and I feel grounded, centered.

What story should I weave today? Cardinal directions give me infinite possibilities; I choose west.

My feet step into the invisible prints they left last week. It's as if the sidewalk is just-soaked sand, preserving a mold of my presence for days to come.

I reach the big intersection, smiling at the familiarity of street names loudly displayed on cobalt signs. *Why are street name signs most commonly in a nature-hued rainbow—greens, blues, whites, browns?* I ponder how I've never pondered this question before, despite walking up to this intersection countless times. Something about today feels new.

My elbow presses into the yellow, dimpled, half-moon button—the city hasn't upgraded this stretch of older crosswalk signals yet—and I inhale the expulsions of metal boxes carrying morning commuters. Smog has started accumulating.

A pixelated man appears on the bottom portion of the signal, and I wonder why he doesn't have shoes. Maybe he's too fleeting: here one minute, gone the next. It's we humans who make strides in the real world; he's just confined to his little black box.

I cross over into the adjacent neighborhood full of more historically preserved quadplexes and futuristic single-family homes. Seeing all these man-made structures makes my mind drift to its sanctuary: nature.

A memory arises. My friend Harry and I are walking through a lush forest near a local park after that day's drizzle. We'd both flown out to Portland from our respective parts of the country to spend a few days exploring a new city and to create un-befored memories.

The ground is spongy beneath us since it never has a chance to dry out. Under the canopy of dense trees, the trail becomes faint as daylight wanes and I spot a large patch of moss. The emerald is too enticing; I walk over and press my hands into the carpet.

"It feels like a cocoon of softness," I tell Harry.

He nods, smiling, and we both lean down to inhale the musk. My lungs expand with freshness and spring.

We walk on, parting the damp silence of evening air, and I close my eyes to see how long I can walk without bumping into something, or scaring myself into opening them.

I imagine a girl with sewing needles on the soles of her big leather boots. She towers above the tree line, branches catching on her amber hair, yet not hindering her assured pace. She ambles steadily across the whole world, familiar with the ephemeral.

She has stories to tell before she goes.

The needles on her boots are abnormally large, almost half her height, and she takes big strides to accommodate their plunge into the earth. Embedded into the rubber soles are the eyelets of these large, metal rods, tethering a red thread through their oval opening. As she walks, the sharp needles till the surface of her path into welcoming soil. Her feet weave a thread of her strides into a delicate, thin tapestry.

With each needle pinprick, she is sowing the seed of each step, sewing the story of her travels right into Earth.

I think of this girl often. The last time was when I was deep in the Verdugo Mountains, just twenty minutes outside of LA. My friend Erica and I had decided to explore a trail unknown to both of us, despite being avid hikers in the Los Angeles area.

Though the sun was hot enough to warrant hiking sans shirts, the fresh, mid-autumn air was just chilly enough to motivate us to keep going, to keep warm.

"Wow, these *hills* just keep going, huh!" Erica exclaimed at the sight of the mountain towering before us.

A steep face, seemingly smooth from a distance, was challenging us to scale it without backsliding on the sandy gravel.

As we walked closer, we saw someone else had carved out small footholds, like irregular steps, to aid in the ascent. These guides from past travelers made me change my usual gait—a long, steady stride—into a stochastic pattern.

Rule number one of climbing a tall mountain: take smaller steps, more often.

And so we climbed upward, sweat dripping from our brow.

What if I had those needles on my hiking boots threading red?

I thought about the kind of stitching I might see beneath my feet.

I want to decorate the whole mountain.

Many miles and hours later, I surveyed our progress, eyeing the delta between the radio towers spearing the mountaintop and the parking lot with our patient cars.

I imagined all the red thread tracing the giant lollipop of our path. Some sideways stitching where Erica and I both hid in the brush to pee; back and forth thread where we found a swing tied to a pine branch and took turns sailing across the sky; a long, uninterrupted swath of thread where I slid down gravel, surfer style.

A Morse code of strides and stops, erratic lines and dots where we took that delicious pause to inhale pacific air.

A story told in footsteps, forever living in the memory of this canyon.

Part of the story unfolded through ordinary routines.

Every few weeks, I'd treat myself to my favorite iced coffee and stroll down the Walk of Fame, emblazoned with stars of celebrities whose names I didn't recognize. That part of Hollywood was grimy, black pavement littered with unrecognizable smears and trash. The stars didn't dazzle there.

But my thread did.

Down Vine and right into the coffee shop on Argyle, my thread had dozens of rows of stitches. It remembered the patterns from countless past strolls and each new coffee walk garnered another layer.

After several years, I could almost sew a fiber pathway. My own red carpet, rolled out to welcome my Chaco-clad feet, the epitome of un-fancy; the epitome of me. It enticed me to sink my hands into ruby hues, enveloping me in a cocooning softness that embraced me in its hold.

Those layers of string from the soles of my shoes made the sidewalk feel well-worn with my presence.

Let me just take my usual route. I've walked this path before.

And it's in these familiar places—the sidewalks with their signature cracks or the mountain ridges whose canyons I know as well as the valleys of my palm—it's in these ritual rhythms I find the most delight.

The thicker my red carpet, the more I can push myself to look for those shining jewels to adorn it.

I'd pass by the vibrant lemon tree in the abandoned yard of the house that burned down last year. Retracing my steps up and down Lexington, I'd ask myself, *What else can I notice?*

Especially during the height of the pandemic lockdowns, my only solace was to wander the streets of my neighborhood, on loops, sewing my shoes' needles into the pavement and leaving a red thread in my wake.

Serendipitously, during this low period, I came across the concept of *flaneuring*: ambling around familiar places with the sole purpose of following one's wonder and curiosity to find pockets of joy.

And so, I did just that.

Where my Chacos graced the ground on Monday, more invisible footprints would later appear. On Tuesday I observed the glint of a green hummingbird. On Wednesday, a dime from 1957. On Thursday, dog poop smeared by an inattentive passerby. On Friday, a yellow-tinted ginkgo leaf. I picked it up and twirled it in my fingers.

Months later, that same leaf would end up inked on my arm. An homage to remember: *Oh, the places I've been!*

All these curiosities, all within one stretch of sidewalk. My red tapestry grew.

And while days were fleeting, each stitch was an invitation to pause and sow a seed for a memory. Bundled together, they wove a story captured in footsteps that would stand the test of time.

I think about ephemerality often. It shows up at 6:23 p.m. on Sundays, as the rejuvenating weekend elegantly curtsies goodbye. Two days to rest never seems enough contrasted with a heavy workload for five.

Ephemerality shows up less frequently as I'm huffing my way up the steepest of inclines or raining crocodile tears swollen with stress.

Hard times pass, slowly. Easy times fly by in an instant.

Our lifetimes, too, are probably the most ephemeral in the cosmic perspective, at least from the anthropocentric point of view. Let's say the average human walks the Earth for seventy-five years. Within the 13.8 billion years the entire universe has existed, a human lifespan is about 5.4×10^{-10} or about .000000000054 percent of the duration of the universe.

I did the math.

We are around for infinitesimally less time than the blink of an eye of a cosmic goddess.

And so, humans have found ways to cope with our brief existence. We have religions promising heaven or hell, beliefs we'll recycle into something or someone else via reincarnation, and practices like meditation that try to firmly ground us in the present.

It sure is nice to have so many options to choose from to help assuage our universal existential crisis.

What I find most interesting is at the core of all these concepts or practices is a seed of a story. A seed that grows to make sense of the absurdity of life and the certainty of death.

Over millennia, this seed sprouts and blooms into a narrative, a story whose tendrils ensnare the hearts and whose honeyed scent finds its way deep into the lungs of millions. A scent for all seasons, fresh with promise.

A story sure does smell like the sweetest flower.

These unique stories, then, be they religious or not, weave a unifying red thread we are tethered to this Earth.

That we belong here, we matter—if only for an instant of time.

The stories of our livelihoods and our travels live forever, woven into single threads or plush red carpets of the sidewalks and trails we call home.

For every step we take—all 216 billion throughout a lifetime—we leave behind a little footprint of us, thread plunged deep into the ground, weaving a tapestry of our adventures.

Wherever we go, there we are. Inscribed into the land eternally.

And so, I weave my own red thread.

I wear leather, rubber-soled boots adorned with giant needles of garnet yarn, walking my way through forests and mountains and cities, leaving my own story on the skin of the Earth.

And when I'm old, on the cusp of vanishing after a lifetime, when that lifetime is but a minuscule tic on the cosmic calendar, there will be something that remains.

I'll look back at the billions of steps I've taken, covering the land in my own red thread.

I'll look back at the life I've sewn, knowing I sowed the seeds for a story well told.

ACKNOWLEDGMENTS

———

Books are never written alone.

Breathing life into *Joy in Plain Sight* was one of the hardest things I've done in my life (so far). From the initial excitement of saying, "Oh my god, I'm actually writing a book!" to the seemingly infinite nights of staring at a screen 'til midnight—we made it.

And it is a deliberate and beautiful *we*, for I could not have done this without my people.

To my partner Nick, whose encouragement kept me going even through the darkest nights. Thank you for your algebraic lessons in story structure, your engulfing hugs, and your incredible patience as you sat down beside me to muddle through murky bits of manuscript. You were—and are—my source of joy and questionable sanity through months of fifteen-hour days. Sneaking in "snugs" with you and our three kitties made every day better. Thanks for being you.

To my family, who cheered me on from three thousand miles away with kind words and "I'm proud of yous." Especially to my mom, who modeled for me her own light, strength, and joy in the little things growing up. "Keep going, girl!" you told me often; thanks for believing in me.

To my sweet, understanding friends, who handled my frazzled or late responses to invites to hang out with grace. As I hermitted away for months to get through long workdays topped with hours of writing, I'm grateful for every text, every phone call, every opportunity to hug one another in person. Y'all mean more than you know. I'm especially grateful to capture the magnificence of a few of these brilliant people as the characters in these stories.

To my beta readers, who read and provided suggestions on several stories each, a love note for each of you:

Dean: Remember that summer night in 2019 sipping our two-dollar beers at South Street when you encouraged me—with raw urgency—to publish an essay on heartbreak? And I submitted it *because you said it was good*? Later you texted me, "One day I'll read your collected essays titled 'Two Dollar Tuesdays.'" While *this* collection of essays bears a different title, your vehement and heartfelt encouragement kept me writing. Thank you for receiving some of my most vulnerable pieces and treating them with such care.

Elliot: To be completely honest, if it wasn't for your text to join you in the writing program—one day before the application closed—I might not have written this book that year! Thanks for making time amid your crazy adventures to provide solid feedback that made my writing better. You've always had that ability to push me beyond my comfort zone, and always with a laugh. I look forward to reading more of your stories and seeing how you'll take over the world someday.

Jon: Here's what I appreciate about you: "Hey so you wanted me to send you my feedback on your writing by the eleventh. Is it okay if I get it to you by the eighth?" Always on time, precise, and insightful—perhaps stemming from our...colorful... consulting days. Thank you for your eagle eye in catching the big and little things and helping me tackle revisions on some of the thorniest sections.

Oksana: Every week without fail, you'd ask me how my book was going during our cross-country phone calls. I don't know where I'd be in this world without you. Thank you for providing such kind words during our conversations, and in the way you made my essays sparkle with your global perspective. How very lucky I am to share this three-decades-long adventure with you, and here's to many more.

Weslee: I think it was a Sunday night. We were sitting on that gray couch, and you said, "Hey remember that time you said you wanted to write a book?" I looked at you quizzically, asking, "Oh, I did?" And then, "Oh. *Oh.* Oh wow. I guess here we are." Thank you for surfacing that nugget of memory that publishing a book was a dream all along. Your feedback was like a warm hug from my favorite sweater.

A tremendous thank you to the entire team at New Degree Press and Creator Institute, Eric Koester, and my terrific editors. I cherished your confidence in me as a writer, and in my meeting deadlines and word count goals and all the other hard things that come with publishing a book. Through your persistent editing and weekly cheerleading, you were my tribe who paved the way for success.

Finally, thank you to the stellar individuals—colleagues past and present, friends, mentors—who supported the book and its sinuous journey and believed in finding the joy in plain sight.

Aditi Gadre
Agrippina Miskevich
Ajibade Olagherr
Alex Landau
Allan Davydov
Amalia Belcher
Amalia McDonald
Ana Mir
Anne McLernon
Ardilla Deneys
Ayla Vo
Ben Dacus
Bobby Alcott
Cheryl Maclean
Christina Ha
Christina Landy
Clifton Jadoo
Cory Welsh
Courtnie Nolan
Dasha Lee
David Goldberger

David Holman
Dean Hansen
Dossier Harps
Elliot Roth
Emily Baxt
Eric Koester
Erica Andreozzi
Erin Sprouse
Felisa Wiley
Fredrick Martin
Gia Orlando
Grant Tate
Gulnara Febres
Hadley Brochu
Harry Rybacki
Hilary Gustave
Irina Davydova
Jack Selby
Jacki Ingros
James Hartsig
Jane Altenhofen

Jane Conner
Jarel Cohen
Javier Soliz
Jess Prom
Jessica Srikantia Field
John Sarvay
Jon Zimmerman
Jonny Grishpul
Joseph Yao
Joshua René
Judy Li
Kris Freeman
Kat Bell
Kaylynn Hill
Kelsey Green
Kelsey Sweeney
Kim Wensel
Kyle Thornburgh
Laura DelPrato
Lee Ann Hennig
Lisa Philyaw
Lisa Safran
Liz Atherton
Lubov Mozolev
Lucia Melgarejo
Marina Naumenko
Matt Palmer
Mike Auerbach
Misha Espinoza
Molly Capriotti
Morgan Lynch
Nani Ross

Neli Vazquez
Nick Krause
Nick Williams
Nora Fallon
Oksana Naumenko
Rachel Glick
Rachel McKeen
Rick Lottenbach
Samantha Lockhart
Sean Sutor
Shane McCarty
Shaun Moshasha
Sky Lucas
Steve Gaines
Steve Hedberg
Susanna Djemileva
Tania Luna
Tatiana Griffin
Thom Morgan
Tojo Thatchenkery
Vanessa Tanicien
Victoria Chen
Victoria Tripsas
Viktor Kozlovskiy
Violette Mahmoudi
Warren Shaeffer
Weslee Heileman
Winston Bonnheim
William Simpson
Zachary Seid

APPENDIX

INTRODUCTION

Goodreads. "Quote by Kurt Vonnegut: 'I Am a Human Being, not a Human Doing.' Accessed October 4, 2021. https://www.goodreads.com/quotes/817241-i-am-a-human-being-not-a-human-doing

LAUGHTER YOGA

Gerloff, Pamela. "You're Not Laughing Enough, and That's No Joke." Psychology Today, June 21, 2011. https://www.psychologytoday.com/us/blog/the-possibility-paradigm/201106/youre-not-laughing-enough-and-thats-no-joke.

Goodreads. "Quote by Michael Pritchard: 'You don't stop laughing because you grow old. You grow old because you stop laughing.' Accessed August 18, 2021. https://www.goodreads.com/quotes/102627-you-don-t-stop-laughing-because-you-grow-old-you-grow.

CAT LESSONS

Bertolucci, Luiz Fernando. "Pandiculation: Nature's Way of Maintaining the Functional Integrity of the Myofascial System?" *Journal of Bodywork and Movement Therapies* 15, no. 3 (July 2011): 268–80. https://doi.org/10.1016/j.jbmt.2010.12.006.

THE CONSTELLATIONS ON OUR SKIN

Rep. *Statistical Yearbook of the Immigration and Naturalization Service, 1999.* Washington, D.C: US Government Printing Office, 2002. https://www.dhs.gov/sites/default/files/publications/Yearbook_Immigration_Statistics_1999.pdf.

"Results of the Diversity Immigrant Visa Program (DV-99)." *US Department of State Office of the Spokesman Press Statement.* US Department of State, May 1998. US Department of State. https://1997-2001.state.gov/briefings/statements/1998/ps980506.html.

EXTREME HAWAIIAN ALOHA

"Cat Litter Products Market Share Analysis Report, 2021-2028." Grand View Research, June 2021. https://www.grandviewresearch.com/industry-analysis/cat-litter-products-market.

Hyatt, Joshua. "Cat Fight." *Inc.*, November 1, 1986. https://www.inc.com/magazine/19861101/2518.html.

ON FINDING JOY WHEN YOU'RE TIRED OF LOOKING

Liang, Lu-Hai. "The Psychology behind 'Revenge Bedtime Procrastination'." BBC Worklife. BBC, November 26, 2020.
https://www.bbc.com/worklife/article/20201123-the-psychol-
ogy-behind-revenge-bedtime-procrastination.

WASHING DISHES

Nhat Hanh, Thich. "Memories from the Root Temple: Washing
Dishes." Plum Village, September 20, 2019.
https://plumvillage.org/articles/memories-from-the-root-
temple-washing-dishes/.

THE SOUND OF SILENCE

Botros, Andrew. "Frequency to Musical Note Converter."
UNSW Music Acoustics, 2001.
https://newt.phys.unsw.edu.au/music/note/.

Cooper, Casey. "US Highway 101." Historic California US Highways, 1999.
http://gbcnet.com/ushighways/US101/index.html.

Spiegel, Alix, Hanna Rosin, and Abby Wendle. "The Last Sound."
NPR, March 8, 2020.
https://www.npr.org/transcripts/821648089.

Suits, B.H. "Tuning: Frequencies for Equal-Tempered Scale, A4
= 440 Hz." Physics of Music - Notes. MIT, 1998.
https://pages.mtu.edu/~suits/notefreqs.html.